This
last
mac

mes
date

THE DEATH OF VENICE

1994

14

THE DEATH OF
VENICE

Stephen Fay
and
Phillip Knightley

ANDRE DEUTSCH

First published 1976 by
André Deutsch Limited
105 Great Russell Street London WC1

Copyright © 1976 by Stephen Fay and Phillip Knightley
All rights reserved

Printed in Great Britain by
Ebenezer Baylis & Son Limited
The Trinity Press, Worcester, and London

ISBN 0 233 96835 0

For our children, Aliya, Kim, Marisa, Matthew
and Susanna, in the hope that they will be
able to see the Venice we know.

Contents

Illustrations

Illustrations

The Loggetta after restoration (*Peter Dunne*)

The interior of the church of San Nicolo dei Mendicoli
(*Sarah Quill*)

Sir Ashley Clarke, Venice in Peril's Venice representative
(*Peter Dunne*)

Venice propped up (*Sarah Quill*)

CHAPTER I

A Sense of Magic

VENICE is like nowhere else in the whole world. It was built where no sensible people would ever put a city, on a series of islands in a shallow, marshy lagoon separating the mainland of Italy from the northern shore of the Adriatic Sea. Its main thoroughfares are canals, its buses are ferries, and its taxis are motorboats. The background noise is not the roar of traffic, but the gentle chug of marine engines and the sound of the wash breaking on the canal sides.

It is difficult to understand why Venice was built where it is when there were safer and drier sites on the mainland; where, for example, the Romans chose to build Altinum. Their empire never extended into the lagoon because it was not until 25 March 421 (according to legend) that Venice was founded. There might be some doubt about the exact date (a Friday, it says in the perpetual calendar of James Morris, that famous chronicler of Venice), but none about the reason. The first Venetians were fleeing from the barbarian armies of Attila the Hun, and Venice was originally a group of islands run from one of them called Torcello. But by the time two enterprising merchants stole the body of St Mark from Alexandria and elevated him into Venice's own patron by naming the great cathedral after him, the centre had shifted south to the island now known as the *centro storico*—the historic centre of Venice.

The islands offered sufficient protection from the barbarians to persuade the early Venetians that it was worth their while putting roots down, abandoning the move back to the mainland, and making the island habitable. When they began to build, it was not only in the great Greco-Roman tradition; they were influenced by the more Oriental patterns of Byzantine art and architecture which the Venetian merchants had observed in Constantinople. (When Venetians sailed down the Adriatic to the Mediterranean they tended to turn to port rather than starboard, for Cyprus and Asia Minor.) Their concentration on commerce seemed to breed a ruthless cunning, and by the twelfth century their island retreat was becoming a significant city-state.

This position was confirmed by a Doge—as the leaders of Venetian government had become known—called Enrico Dandolo. He agreed to transport the Frankish armies of the Fourth Crusade to the Holy Land for the glory of God— plus 85,000 marks and half the booty. When it became clear that the Franks did not have enough marks, they were persuaded to pay their debt by using their armies to take Constantinople in the name of Venice. By the thirteenth century the tentacles of Venice had reached out further than any other city's—Marco Polo had even reached China by the overland route—and Venice was 'lord and master of a quarter and a half quarter of the Roman Empire'.

A century later the tourist trade had already begun. The square in front of St Mark's was filled with visitors from Asia, Africa and western Europe, and they would still recognize many of the buildings on today's tourist routes. The healthy profits made by monopoly trading with the

Venetian empire were used to build the great *palazzi*, the churches and the public buildings, first in the Byzantine style, then in the Gothic, which had spread west to Venice. Finally, the Palladian, which was indigenously Venetian, and the Baroque took over, and Venice was rich enough to have fine examples of enough architectural styles to make it into a living museum of European architecture. It was no longer a mere city-state but the *Serenissima Republicca*—the most Serene Republic. By the fifteenth century visitors were already beguiled by the sights and bemused by the warren of canals, bridges and alleys. Shakespeare knew all about it when he described the route to Shylock's house in the *Merchant of Venice*: 'Turn up on your right hand at the next turning, but at the next turning of all, on your left; marry, at the very next turning of no hand but turn down indirectly to the jew's house.' Venetians overcame this problem by standardizing the advice they offer to visitors: '*sempre diritto*', they say, 'straight ahead'.

During the Renaissance a group of great painters made up the Venetian school. Bellini, Carpaccio, Titian and Tintoretto all produced an astonishing volume of work, and much of it stayed in the buildings for which it was originally painted. Venice had become immensely powerful, and remarkably beautiful, but it was not so powerful that it could retain a monopoly on exploration. It did not initiate its own decline; that was done by Vasco da Gama's voyage round the Cape, his opening of the sea route to the East, which was to end Venice's commercial monopolies. Once the decline began, the Venetians were incapable of stopping it; perhaps for that reason they determined to enjoy it.

James Morris observes of this period that 'the carnivals of the Venetian decadence were seen from the start as a useful tourist attraction—and the more decadent they became, the more people flocked to them.' The prostitutes became as famous as the architecture. A contemporary report in the eighteenth century suggested that the objective of Venetian domestic policy was 'to encourage idleness and luxury in the nobility, to cherish ignorance and licentiousness in the clergy, to keep alive continual faction in the common people, and to connive at viciousness and debauchery in the convents.' The physical effect was to make the city, if anything, even more gorgeous.

Napoleon thought Venice significant enough to commemorate its defeat in 1797 on the triumphal arch he had built in front of the Louvre in Paris. But his victory was so easy that the city remained unmarked by the battle. The government of the Republic simply voted itself out of existence, by 512 to 30 votes, with 5 abstentions. Napoleon handed it over to the Austrians, who governed it with some success, partly because they also loved Venice, though they did cause its demise as an island by building the causeway from the mainland in 1846. When Venice finally became part of the new Italian state in 1866, Rome mostly ignored it. Its commercial power had withered away, and its political power had disappeared.

But Venice never lost the power to hypnotize the traveller who came to it across the lagoon. To the massive populations of the new industrial powers, it became an extraordinary revelation of things past, the greatest tourist attraction in the world. 'Venice commands emotions inspired by no other place;' writes James Morris, 'a sense of magic still, as though one has been wandering through ethereal back canals; a sense of release from the ordinary or logical; a sense of ill-explained but ecstatic yearning; and a blurred perception of the absolute that is art, nature, surprise, pathos, intricacy, triumph and melancholy all mixed up.' Now Venice is dying and there is no hope of saving her. This book is an account of that death, and an indictment of those responsible for it.

CHAPTER 2

A Pattern of Decay

ONE of Venice's virtues is that it is like a great museum which is, at the same time, lived in. This brings the whole range of its architecture and its paintings alive; they are being *used* instead of *housed*. But since it began to die, Venice has become a very difficult city to inhabit; so difficult that tens of thousands of Venetians have had enough, and moved out. The population statistics are striking. In 1950 there were 184,447 people in the historic centre. In each five-year period after that the number fell by approximately 20,000, until, by 1965, it was 123,733. In 1970 it was 111,550, and for the first time there were more 'Venetians' living on the mainland, on the 'terrafirma', than in Venice itself. By 1974 the population was only 105,656. In a world of exploding cities, Venice is one of the very few that is not.

The main reason why 78,791 Venetians left their city is contained in a housing study undertaken in 1957. It reached the following dismal conclusions: two-thirds of the housing studied required radical restoration; nearly half was in mediocre condition; one-sixth was in extremely bad condition, and three houses in every hundred constituted a public danger. About a quarter of Venetian housing was crowded, with more than two people living in every room. Nine houses in every hundred were uninhabitable. Half the homes depended on the kitchen for heating—only one-tenth of the houses in that damp city had central heating. Eleven in a hundred apartments were never exposed to the sun and thirty-eight in a hundred were exposed to it only minimally.

Things have improved since then, partly because living standards have risen, and partly because of the exodus, which obviously reduced overcrowding. But they have not improved enough to break the progression of decay. When people leave there is no longer any need for so many churches, so they are closed or deconsecrated. There are fewer workers available, so museums close too; at first in the off-season, then for certain days, and finally for ever.

Venice is a city beset by misfortune, suffering from severe neglect, caught in a cycle that is destroying her. Because she has been neglected, fewer of her citizens want to live there. Because fewer Venetians want to live in Venice there is less urgency to remedy the neglect—nearly two out of every three buildings need attention. The results of this cycle can be seen everywhere. A short tour of the city will not only serve to show how pollution, water and weather are attacking it but will also offer some key examples of what ought to be seen soon, before it crumbles away, or is closed for good. The exhibits are listed in a particular order which allows a visitor to Venice, armed with a good map, to start at the railway station and, by walking in a clockwise direction, to see them all. (The tour is inspired by Guilio Lorenzetti, author of *Venice and Its Lagoon*, incomparably the most complete guidebook in a field in which there has been much excellent competition.) A canvas displayed at the National Gallery in London shows the view Canaletto had from the bridge across the Grand Canal, near to where Venice railway station now stands; a comparison of the Canaletto and the view today is depressing.

The Scalzi, on the right, is one of the more modern churches in Venice; completed in 1689, it is a good and unusual example of Baroque architecture. The Scalzi is unlucky: the ceiling painted by Tiepolo, the most colourful and fluent of Venetian painters, was destroyed by an Austrian bomb in 1915, and the statues on the façade are so heavily encrusted with the excretion of flocks of pigeons as to be barely visible. Pieces of the statues frequently fall on the busy pavement outside the church, so a barrier has been placed around it, and a covered arcade built to the front door to allow worshippers to enter to praise God without being injured by falling masonry on the way.

The church of San Simeone Piccolo, across the Grand Canal, was completed shortly before Canaletto painted the scene, and is easily recognized by its high copper dome. It was much criticized by Giulio Lorenzetti for its ungraceful and disproportionate shape, but the great English artist, J. M. W. Turner, liked it well enough to paint it as well. Lorenzetti's criticisms cannot be properly put to the test, however, because the church has been declared unsafe to enter, and is now closed.

To see a pleasant row of *palazzi* beyond the Scalzi and the monastery, it is necessary to consult Canaletto, because they were knocked down to make way for the railway station, built by the Austrians after they had completed the causeway. But not even the nineteenth-century station survives. In 1951 another station was built—long, low, white, and entirely out of character.

In the Cannaregio district, an area of much poor housing, the spire of the fourteenth century Gothic church of San

Alvise lost its point in a thunderstorm some years ago; what is left will fall down if not repaired. It would not be the first or the grandest to go, but its loss would diminish the Venetian skyline seen during the journey by boat across the lagoon from Marco Polo airport.

The Scuola Grande della Misericordia has one of those vast, ugly brick faces that are normally hidden behind a façade. When it was built the greatest Venetian architect, Andrea Palladio, designed a detailed façade for it, but it was never executed. It was originally built as a meeting hall for a Venetian *scuola*, or religious guild, in 1583, shortly before Sir Walter Raleigh tried to colonize Virginia, and five years before the Spanish Armada. Now it is a municipal storehouse —and a basketball arena. As such it is a remarkable sight, with traces of *trompe l'oeil* decoration still visible on the walls behind the seats. Even this unusual use of a stately building will not continue for much longer, because the Scuola Grande della Misericordia is fast becoming unsafe. Its walls are crumbling, and the cost of restoring it is greater than the Venetian passion for basketball would justify.

Santa Maria dei Miracoli is a lovely little church with a beautifully restored statue of a Virgin and Child above the front entrance. It was built in the fifteenth century, and ruined in the twentieth. The interior is decorated with marble, much of it left over from St Mark's Cathedral; there is a staircase leading to the altar, and the natural light is so good that it is easy to see what has gone wrong. On the base of the pulpit the marble is crumbling away; worse still, the marble walls are encrusted with growing patches of white salt. Yet the Miracoli was only recently restored, and that, sadly, is the trouble. Excessive moisture was damaging the church. A damp course was installed, but the marble was replaced before the walls had been allowed to dry properly. The result was to trap hundreds of kilos of salt in the walls, and now this has started to destroy the marble from the inside.

The Scuola di San Marco abuts the great Gothic church of San Giovanni e Paolo. There are always people bustling in and out because the fifteenth-century guildhall is now Venice's main hospital. The façade makes it possible not just to observe the destruction of the city, but to feel it too. At the far end of the Scuola's façade there is a relief statue of three turbaned men set in one of the decorative stone perspectives. At head height there is a ledge, and anyone running their fingers along it will find them covered in dust and fragments of stone, daily physical proof of the speed of its erosion. The stone carving above the door of the hospital, although recently restored, is already flaking away. The church is plagued by pigeons. They have nested in a roof that was in no fit state to house them. It leaks badly and the plaster falls away from the ceiling during bad storms.

The Palazzo Gritti-Contarini-Morosini in the Campo San Francesco—near the gasworks—is arguably the most striking and beautiful slum property in Europe. It was built in 1525, and became the Venetian residence of the Papal Nuncio until the middle of the nineteenth century. Then it was taken over by the state, which immediately covered its frescoes with a coat of whitewash. Now its four arched windows above the balcony have been bricked in, and a heating exhaust pipe sticks out from the room where generations of cardinals went about their business.

The Palazzo Zorzi, a second decaying *palazzo*, is best seen from the back garden of the Trattoria al Giardinetto, a noisy bar populated largely by men playing a Venetian variety of bowls. The owners of the Palazzo said they were prepared to restore it if they were given permission to convert it into apartments. Permission was refused and now the Palazzo's rear wall is steadily crumbling away.

St Mark's Cathedral looks substantial enough but its guardians, including one known as the *proto*, who is specially charged with the care of the fabric, are fighting a losing battle. Groups of skilled craftsmen work continually in the building; like painting the Forth Bridge, or cleaning the windows in a skyscraper, the work is never done, and St Mark's is always falling further behind.

Underneath any of the five arches along the façade, pale sections in the otherwise blackened stone shows where whole areas of the decorated archways have crumbled away. The problem has been so embarrassing that the *proto* has some-times ordered workmen onto ladders to paint the pale marks black, presumably on the basis that what the eye does not see . . . A survey of the stone in the arches in the summers of 1973 and 1975 was alarming. Above the main entrance, for example, a series of groups showing Venetian craftsmen include, on the right, carpenters. In 1973 it was possible to identify their tools, but it was not so two years later, and never will be again. They have crumbled away. This is happening, too, on the great central arch with the angel at its peak, rising high above the doorways and the bronze horses. It is this arch, and the five Byzantine domes behind it, which set St Mark's apart from other cathedrals in Europe, and make it possible to understand why mediaeval and Renaissance Venice was regarded as the cultural and com-mercial hinge between east and west. On the arches them-selves the decay is less noticeable than it is lower down, but the accumulation of detail will inevitably be lost.

Inside the Cathedral, at the end of the lobby or atrium, is a small room called the Zen Chapel after a fifteenth-century cardinal who left a substantial legacy to the Venetian Republic, and had his reward on earth as well as in heaven by having his sarcophagus placed in so prominent a position. At the bottom of the columns on the altar there are piles of marble dust which has fallen to the floor; at the join between the stone and the metal altar top, one can see the bright green stain of copper chloride which is eating the metal away. The mosaics on either side of the altar are falling apart because the plaster holding the decorative pieces in place is crumbling.

On one side of the great altar is a small chapel housing the altar of St Paul. On the left of the chapel is a stone panel which looks as if it is being restored because the bottom half is pale in colour and the top half is a deeper brown. In fact, the line between the two marks the point to which condensation has risen in the wall, and the pale area which looks as though it has been cleaned is actually disintegrating.

The Venetian Gothic Palazzo Fortuny is a municipally-owned museum of costume design, housing the collection of Fortuny himself—one of the most famous twentieth-century designers—and various other odds and ends. But like many other municipal buildings in Venice, it is visibly falling apart. At its present rate of decay, the Palazzo Fortuny and its collection will soon be closed.

Churches seem to suffer most. In the Campo Santa Margherita, at the base of what remains of the old campanile, is the entrance to a cinema which specializes in blue movies, shown in the body of the old church. It is not the only church in Venice to have changed its use, though none quite so dramatically. The decrepit church of Angelo Raffaele has a façade which seems to be held together by two vast First World War memorials. The interior has paintings by

Guardi, among others, but it is dark and dank and few people come to see them. There is a large lozenge shaped hole in the plaster at the top right hand corner of the domed ceiling. Unless it is fixed the fabric will deteriorate further, and the paintings will have to be removed.

The church of Santa Teresa is closed now, and it is necessary to ask the priest, Father Scarpi, or a nun in the mothers' home behind the large green door next to the church, for admission. It is best seen when the clouds are low over Venice, and the light is poor. The rain does not just drip steadily through holes in the roof; it pours in through a broken window above the main altar, a very nice piece of marble, decorated with lapis lazuli and virtually impossible to move to a safer place. Lorenzetti describes Santa Teresa as 'seventeenth-century architecture with a rich façade. The spacious cloister, its beautiful spacious arcades, mostly built in unfortunately, is still preserved.' It sounds worth preserving, but in 1975 it had deteriorated so badly that Father Scarpi concluded that it was too uncomfortable for the children's Sunday school to be held there, and that it would not be long before it was not just uncomfortable but dangerous as well.

Santa Teresa's virtues are those of most seventeenth-century Venetian churches. The nave is cube shaped, with excellent proportions, and if there were still paintings—instead of just their cracked wooden backing, through which the sky shows clearly—and the decorations on the walls were less faint, it would be most pleasant to look at. There are more altars spaced at intervals around the church, each with a thick pile of marble dust at its base. The priest points to one of them and speaks wistfully of a Madonna and Child that had been part of a decorative inlay where now there is only

CHAPTER 3

The Great Flood

AT 10 pm on 3 November 1966, as the whole of Northern Italy was lashed by gale force winds, the evening high tide in Venice reached its peak. The tide was higher than average, but nothing to worry about—the water would soon begin to ebb; low tide would occur between 4 am and 5 am, then the sea would begin to flow back again; a sequence well understood and entirely predictable, an immutable law of astronomical science. But at 5 am the unbelievable had occurred —the tide had remained high. The first alarm went up, and dawn saw the more prudent Venetians emptying their shops, preparing duckboards and securing their boats. Towards noon, the first high tide was swollen by the arrival of the second. The waters spilled over the canal banks. St Mark's Square went under, leaving the Ducal Palace, the Cathedral and all the monuments which surround the square peering above the water like a renascent Atlantis. The electricity supply failed, telephones went dead. The water was soon too deep to wade through, and in the light rain and the strong but warm *scirocco* wind, a few boats battled their way along the streets and across the squares.

In one way it was just as well the telephones were not working. Across from the city, on the long narrow strip of land that protects the lagoon from the Adriatic, events so unprecedented were occurring that if they had been known of in Venice everyone might well have fled in panic. At Pellestrina huge waves pounded the massive *murazzi*, the stone sea walls built late in the eighteenth century to keep the Adriatic at bay, smashing free huge blocks of marble and flinging them aside like pebbles, until the walls cracked, and then collapsed, and the water rushed in. On wider stretches of the peninsula the sea rose and covered the land until the Adriatic and the lagoon became one. Cavalino, an area of orchards, vineyards, and farmland disappeared under 15 feet high waves, drowning cattle, sweeping away agricultural machinery and forcing the people to their roofs, or to flee in boats and rafts. The islands of Pellestrina and Saint Erasmo were completely submerged. By nightfall five thousand people were homeless and seeking shelter in ships, hospitals and military barracks.

Venice, by now in absolute darkness at the end of the short November day, knew none of this. It waited for the crucial hour of 6 pm, the second and last ebb tide. If the water failed to recede then, clearly supernatural forces were at work; a sense of foreboding, a doomsday atmosphere, infected many Venetians. Huddled around transistor radios in candlelight they heard the 5 pm news announcement that storms had caused severe damage in northern Italy, floods in Florence and then, to the listeners' amazement, 'high tide in St Mark's Square'. The Venetians had barely recovered from the shock of hearing that the rest of Italy appeared to have abandoned them when it became clear that the tide was not about to ebb. On the contrary, at the very moment it should have turned, it began to rise again. The water was now so high that the waves whipped by the wind were breaking on the arches of the Ducal Palace. Perhaps the most terrifying thing was that apart from the lapping of the water, the apparent death of Venice was proceeding in silence and total darkness.

Then at 9 pm the wind dropped, and soon afterwards the water began to go down. It left the city as it had entered it, suddenly and violently. It had reached the unprecedented height of 6½ feet above normal high level and had caused at least 40 billion lire (£26 million)* worth of damage. Now Venetians came down from the safety of their upper storeys to inspect this ruin—oil stains everywhere, mattresses, smashed furniture, broken-backed gondolas, muck, filth, dead pigeons, rats and cats strewn in the squares and streets; slowly at first, and then from every quarter, the flicker of hundreds of tiny flames were seen as Venetians went around their stricken city by candlelight. When they met, they all said the same thing—that if the wind had not dropped, and a third high tide had entered the lagoon to boost the two already there, then quite likely Venice would not have survived. Yet, in keeping with that first ludicrously inadequate report on Italian radio—'high tide in St Mark's Square'—the disaster in Venice went unremarked for almost a week, not only by Italy, but by the rest of the world.

There were two reasons for this. At the same time as the lagoon overwhelmed Venice, further south the river Arno, swollen by the opening of sluice gates to save an upstream dam from bursting, broke its banks and swirled through Florence. The Uffizi, the National Library, the State Archives, the Bargello, the Cathedral, the Baptistry, Santa Maria Novella, Santa Croce, and countless other churches,

* All sums in lire have been converted at a rate of 1,500 to the £. Until the collapse of the lire in 1976 the commonest rate against the US dollar was 660 lire, e.g. 1 billion = $150 million.

museums and historic buildings were filled with water, mud, fuel oil and sewage. In the rush to save the immense artistic wealth of Florence, Venice was virtually forgotten. Also, Venice appeared to recover rapidly. Within three weeks, Florians—the oldest surviving café in St Mark's Square— had reopened, its richly upholstered chairs and furnishings dried out, the only obvious signs of the disaster the tell-tale high water marks on walls stained black with oil. It was not until the following summer that it gradually became apparent that the damage to Venice had been much more profound, much more permanent, much more tragic than anyone had imagined. 'On that single night of the floods,' the Mayor said, 'our city aged fifty years.'

The 1966 floods finally brought home to the world what had been happening in Venice: the catalogue of its ailments was alarming. The major danger was from the city's age-old enemy, the sea. The ancient Venetians had come to terms with the fact that their city, only inches above high tide level, could be at the mercy of the Adriatic. By maintaining the natural balance of the lagoon—the free flow of tides and the shape and character of the islands and foreshores—and by taking great care of the city's seaward defences, the great dikes or sea walls, they had always been able to live with the exceptional storm and the occasional flood. The disaster in 1966 was evidence that all this had somehow changed. What had gone wrong?

To begin with, the maintenance of the sea walls had been neglected, and when they were most needed they collapsed. Next, the precious few inches between high water in the lagoon and street level in Venice had been critically reduced. Because of the melting of the polar ice-caps, the level of the Adriatic has been rising by about one centimetre every ten years. At the same time, the whole basin of the River Po, of which Venice is a part, has been sinking about ten times as fast. Some of this sinking is natural and inevitable, but it has

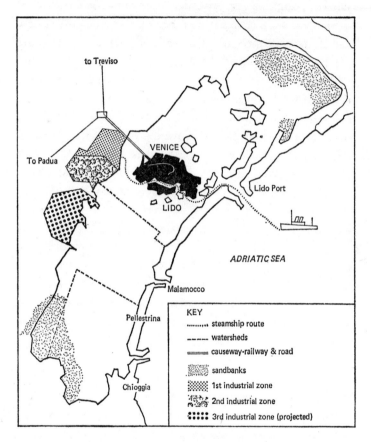

been accelerated by the extraction of fresh water from the subsoil of Venice for use in the huge industrial development at Porto Marghera, on the mainland behind the historic centre of the city.

This same industrial development, and the prosperity that

it has brought Venice, are the other factors that have upset the city's defences. Industry needed land for expansion, docks to unload its raw materials, and increasingly bigger ships to bring them in. It has disturbed the natural balance of the lagoon with reclamation schemes, the dredging of new and deeper channels, and the wash of giant ships. Its waste products have polluted the water and its fumes the air, and they have combined and reinforced each other to deal the death blow. Venice floods more frequently because her defences have been run down. The flood waters contain not only sea salt, which can be damaging enough, but chemical pollution as well. The polluted flood water enters the structure of Venetian buildings and creeps through their walls, until they decay; and canals that were once overlooked by some of the finest houses in Europe now offer access instead to mile after mile of rotting beauty. The polluted air attacks the stone of the city's sculpture, eating away the fine detail and then consuming the marble at an ever-increasing pace until it crumbles to dust. By the time this effect had even been noticed, much less had something done about it, it was already too late to save the best of Venice's sculpture. It may be too late to save anything now.

After the 1966 floods the Italian government quickly agreed to provide about 8 billion lire ($£5\frac{1}{2}$ million) for repairing and strengthening Venice's sea walls. A group of Dutch engineers was invited to see what further defences could be built, and, most promising of all, UNESCO became involved. At its own suggestion it undertook to organize a common effort to help Venice on the grounds that the city's future was not only the concern of Italy but of all Western civilization—'Venice is a moral obligation on the international community.' Following UNESCO's initiative there sprang up a number of national organizations all dedicated to helping the city, such as Venice in Peril in Britain; Save Venice Inc. in the United States; Comité Français pour la Sauvegarde de Venise in France; Arbeitskreis Venedig der Deutschen Unesco-Kommission in Germany; Venezia Nostra and many other groups in Italy; in all some thirty-four organizations in fourteen countries.

It was an impressive response, and for a brief period the future of Venice again looked almost as bright as it had done in the heyday of the Serene Republic. Then everything began to go wrong. Anxious not to appear to be interfering in the internal affairs of a member state, UNESCO made the mistake of standing aside to allow Rome to get on with the job of saving Venice. Unfortunately, the nature of the Italian constitution and the tradition and temperament of Italian politicians was such that Rome was incapable of getting on with the job, but entirely capable of making certain that no one else could get on with it either. So in the ten years since Venice's peril was first fully realized there have been reports and counter-reports, conferences, competitions, speeches, meetings, tours of inspection, promises and plans, but no action. A Special Law was passed to save Venice, but not implemented. An international loan of £200 million was raised to save Venice, but the money never arrived. The national organizations raised and sent money to restore Venice: the Italian government levied a tax on it. Governments rose and fell, committees were formed and disbanded, scientists and technicians, art and sculpture specialists did experiments and made recommendations. The government ignored them all. During this ten-year period it became obvious that there was a force at work beyond that usually encountered in organizing an operation as large and as costly as that needed to save Venice, namely the malaise of present-day democratic government, not only in Italy but elsewhere as well: the men who had the power to save Venice were not prepared to take responsibility for the decision; the men who were prepared to take responsibility did not have the power. And Venice, probably in a more tragic form than anywhere else, posed a question Western society is reluctant to face: how much of its present affluence is it prepared to sacrifice to conserve the glories of its past? Modern Venice includes not only the historic centre but the huge, ugly, space-age development at Marghera; not only the *palazzi* on the canals but the modern workers' flats in the sprawling dormitory suburb of Mestre; and the interests of these two 'other Venices' are in direct conflict with those of the historic centre. Venice is a victim of undisciplined industrial progress and deliberate neglect, and if we are to understand why it is too late to save her then we need to go back to when this neglect first began.

CHAPTER 4

The Case History

THE lagoon in which Venice stands is the result of the retreat of the Adriatic from its peak during the Pliocene Age, more than a million years ago. What is now known as Italy then consisted of not much more than the Alps and the Apennines, and the Adriatic stretched inland as far as Turin. The sea receded, and with lavish over-reaction went back so far that many of the present Italian islands became part of the mainland. As recently as classical Roman times, there was, for example, a flourishing seaside resort six miles out to sea from the present resort of Lignano. As the sea slowly crept in again, it met silt carried down from the mainland by three rivers: the Brenta, the Piave, and the Sile. Gradually, a lagoon of about 210 square miles was formed. It consists of a complicated network of natural channels connected with each other and with the sea, dotted with islands and mud-flats, which are exposed at low tide. The foreshore is marshy, the water is generally shallow and the lagoon is open to the Adriatic through three main breaks in the 25-mile long bar of narrow land that runs along the seaward side—the Lido, Malamocco and Chioggia channels.

The early Venetians understood the workings of this lagoon, came to terms with it, and were careful not to disturb it more than was necessary. The regular ebb and flow of the tides provided them with an excellent sewage and rubbish disposal system. Twice each day the tide receded across the lagoon and into the Adriatic, taking with it the effluent from Venice's canals, and twice daily it returned bringing the fresh and sweet-smelling sea. Unusually high tides spent themselves on the *barene*, the mudflats, or were mopped up by marshy swamps behind Venice. But occasionally a disaster occurred.

As early as 589 AD, a chronicle recalls, 'The waters changed their usual course and the whole land took on the appearance of a marsh. The inundation lasted an extremely long time, and the people said, "non in terra neque in aqua sumus nos viventes" [we are living neither on land nor on the water]'. In 885 there was a report of water 'invading the whole city, penetrating the houses and the churches,' and in 1250 'the water rose from eight o'clock until midday. Many were drowned inside their houses or simply died of the cold.'

So in the fourteenth century the Venetians decided to strengthen the seaward defences of their lagoon, and they built the first walls to keep out the Adriatic. True, they were made of little more than clay and wickerwork and needed replacing every few years, but it was a beginning; and when two rough seas in 1686 and 1691 swept them totally away the natural next step was to consider some solid, permanent structure. On 24 April 1744 the first stone of a massive sea defence system was laid, and the first section was successfully finished in 1751. The Venetian Senate now became obsessed with the scheme. Money was no object, no material too good, and no artisan too skilled as the dying Republic poured out its patrimony on its seaward defences. On one small section alone it spent a sum equivalent to some £10 million. Ships ran to and from the quarries of Istria bringing great marble blocks which were cut, fitted and bound with mortar by *i sassanti*, the stone men, who lived in great numbers along the coast. The work took thirty-nine years, a monument to the Republic's concern for Venice's future. On the section at Pellestrina a commemorative tablet read 'The Guardians of the Water have set this colossal mole of solid marble against the sea so that the sacred estuaries of the city and the Seat of Liberty may be eternally preserved.'

The Republic fell to Napoleon in 1797, but the Austrians, inheriting Venice from France, recognized the importance of the sea walls, repaired them when they cracked under heavy seas in 1825 and between 1836 and 1846 allocated two million Austrian lire (the equivalent of about £1 million a year) for maintenance work alone, adding about 15,000 tons of marble a year as reinforcement. But under the government of a united Italy work tapered off. In 1907 a law was passed to protect Italy's coastline from erosion. Under this law, sea defence work could be financed only if it was near urban settlements—a precaution against big landowners getting government money to protect valuable but sparsely populated holdings. But since the greater part of the Venetian sea walls were *not* near urban settlements, they were excluded from an allocation under the 1907 Act. Furthermore, the care of the land strip, including the sea walls, was now divided between the Ministry of Agriculture and the Ministry of Public Works. Venice found itself trapped by bureaucratic definitions and inter-departmental rivalry and was starved of funds. Work on the sea walls was first reduced to an absolute minimum and then virtually abandoned. By the 1960s the ludicrous situation was reached in which the Italian government was spending an average of only one dollar a yard per year to maintain Venice's sea wall defences.

The diminishing desire to maintain the walls was symptomatic of a changed attitude to the lagoon itself. Throughout history, caring Venetians have fought for their lagoon against those who have wanted to conquer and exploit it. The historian Roberto Cessi has described how thirteenth-century Venetians, alarmed at the growth of dams, barricades, and fish traps, took political action to ensure that the basic balance of the lagoon, on which the life of the city depended, should not be endangered by urban growth.

Under first the Magistrato del Proprio, then the Magistratura delta del Piovego (Rain and Water Authority) and finally, in 1501, the Magistratura alle Acque (the Water Authority), a 'zone of respect' was created around Venice, in which any reclamation or barricade was prohibited.

Sometimes, those Italians who considered the agricultural problems of the mainland more important than the water problems of the lagoon managed to sneak through a reclamation scheme before the authorities could act, but generally the 'zone of respect' succeeded in maintaining the lagoon's balance until twentieth-century industrialization caught up with it.

At the height of its power, Venice had deliberately confined its industry to the island for strategic reasons. It is said the Venetian secret service would seek out and murder any Murano glass blower who left so that he could not reveal the secrets of Venetian glass manufacture. Apart from trade and commerce, the biggest single employer in Venice was the Arsenale, the munitions factory and shipyard, which gave Dante his vision of hell. When it collapsed in 1916, thousands of Venetians were thrown out of work.

One of the men who sought to cushion that blow was Count Giuseppe Volpi. Volpi saw that Venice's geographical position could be turned to good use in the industrial era. Taking advantage of Venice's port facilities, large-scale industry could make goods for northern Italy and Central Europe, and since the factories would employ local labour, Venice's unemployment problems would be solved. Volpi saw however that industrial development on this scale would ruin the city he loved, so on the advice of a prominent hydrologist, Professor Coen Cagli, he sited the nucleus of the development at Porto Marghera on the mainland, well away from the historic centre; the workers would travel to and from the factories across the causeway.

The idea was economically sound; industrialists were offered land at exceptionally advantageous terms, and *The Times* correspondent was soon warning English tourists that, as their train approached Venice, they would see 'docks and factories in the course of construction . . . a new industrial port destined to raise Venice once more to a position of primary importance among the ports of the Mediterranean.'

At the beginning industry was still small enough in scale for control to be retained locally. To make sure that remained so, the city boundaries were extended in 1926 so that Porto Marghera was absorbed into Venice proper. During Mussolini's dictatorship, the new port grew quickly, partly because Count Volpi was a power in the land, and could nudge industry towards his pet project on the edge of the lagoon. It survived the Second World War, for Venice was not an Allied target (the main rail centres, which were, lay inland). After the war, the future Volpi had dreamed of for Porto Marghera finally came true.

Venice is the closest major port in Western Europe to the

Middle East (the reason, after all, for its power from the thirteenth to the seventeenth century). It was natural that, as Europe's demand for oil grew greedily after the war, Porto Marghera should grow with it.

In the race for expansion, the dangers to the balance of the lagoon were now forgotten. Marghera nudged up to the lagoon's edges and, when no one protested, swallowed whole areas. No request for the reclamation of an inlet, a sandbar, a marsh, went unsatisfied. The so-called first and second industrial zones reclaimed 3,830 acres from the lagoon. Montecatini and SAVA set up the two largest alumina and aluminium plants in Italy. Ilva built large steel works. Vetrocoke, ammonia, nitric acid and fertilizer plants were established, as well as ship building yards, electrometal-lurgical and calcium carbide works. An international airport was built on reclaimed land at Tessera, and still more land was reclaimed for agricultural use.

In the 1950s Montedison (Italy's ICI or Dupont), announced that it would build one of the largest petrochemical complexes in Europe, the first stage of a vast new industrial expansion. Montedison chemical works had been built on the second industrial zone. But the authorities now decided that there must be a third zone of nearly 10,000 acres, and they started to reclaim the land for this early in the 1960s.

The lagoon had by now become an empty space that only had to be filled in to provide cheap land. As one industrialist said, it was 'good building water'. There was even a suggestion that the lagoon be dammed into three parts. One would be within a line drawn from Fusina on the mainland to one end of the Lido, and one would be within a line from the airport to Saint Erasmo. The third part would comprise the historic centre of Venice, which would still be connected to the sea by a greatly reduced lagoon opening through the Lido. The two flanking sections could then be filled in, paved over, and developed for industry and housing, leaving Venice an island in a sea of factories and workers' flats.

This radical change in attitude to the lagoon brought changes to the people of Venice. Count Volpi thought that Marghera would become 'the lungs of Venice', breathing modern commercial life into the city from a decorous distance. The poor would work on the docks at 12 lire a day, and then return at night to their beautiful but uncomfortable houses in the historic centre.

It did not work out that way. Transport was inconvenient and expensive and, with eminent good sense, many workers preferred a modern warm, dry flat on the mainland to a picturesque but cold and damp residence in the centre of Venice. The result was that alongside the industrial centre of Porto Marghera there grew rapidly the sprawling dormitory suburb of Mestre, a jumble of crowded apartment buildings and offices which has contributed heavily to the change that has taken place in the character of Venice. To begin with, the historic centre, that part the tourists call 'Venice', has become only a small part of the municipality of Venice. The population of the municipality at the last official count was 365,000 but less than one third of these 'Venetians' lived in the historic centre, and more than half in Mestre and Porto Marghera. Venetian councillors may meet in a palace in the historic centre but many then cross the causeway back to Mestre where they live and where most of their political support comes from. Power in local politics has swung heavily away from the historic centre to the industrial area. And as Venetian workers moved to Mestre—even those whose jobs were still in the historic centre seemed to prefer to live outside it and commute in—the rich of Europe moved in.

The original working-class population of Venice began to be replaced by a wealthier class, seeking a prestige residence or even a second house—Milanese industrialists, for example. This explains the phenomenon of the increasing average age of the residents of the historic centre—it is now over forty—and the fact that it has the lowest birth rate in Italy. A recent study by three Venetian sociologists concluded:

> The relatively high costs of the transformation and maintenance of the heritage of Venetian buildings automatically select according to the rigid logic of a market economy, the users capable of supporting them, and accelerate the process of expulsion, not only of the working class, but also of the middle class and of young couples whose budget is modest. The end result has been to make Venice a city of the very young, the very old and the very rich.

As well as causing political and demographic upheavals, the industrial development at Porto Marghera also produced profound physical changes. Chemical discharges polluted the sea and the air. Factories sank bores and pumped water from underground, upsetting the foundations on which Venice rests. More and deeper canals were dredged for more and bigger ships, until one ship per hour, day and night, was passing Venice en route to Marghera. Reclamation had removed the marshy shore, one of the important buffers to abnormally high tides. The balance of the lagoon was disturbed, and Venice paid for it.

In the 100 years before the great floods of 1966, there had

been 54 *acque alte* (high waters) in Venice. In the first 50 of these 100 years, there were only 7 floods; in the last 35 years of the period there were 48 floods, and no fewer than 30 of these occurred in the final 10 years. Lesser flooding—water nevertheless high enough to cover the pavements—occurred 295 times in the period 1972–74, an increase of 80 per cent over 1962–64. That is the measure of the acceleration. Nearly 15 per cent of the population of Venice now live at—not above, or slightly above, but *at*—water level.

Apart from the misery and immediate economic loss this flooding causes it has other, more dangerous, long-term effects. Although it appears to be built of solid stone, Venice is actually 90 per cent brick, faced with stucco to give an illusion of stone. Brick is a very porous material, taking in water and carrying it by capillary action. The early Venetians were well aware of this. Their houses and palaces are built on a foundation of short wooden piles, about seven feet by eight inches, mostly made from oak from Dalmatia. These were driven into the clay by hand by several labourers hoisting a drop hammer under the orders of a master site-driver, who kept time with a chanted singsong that has become part of Venetian folklore. On top of the piles, the builder constructed a platform of several layers of planks, and on this the first course of bricks was laid. When the brickwork reached paving level, the builders then inserted one or two courses of Istrian stone, quarried from the Istrian peninsula that faces Venice on the opposite shore of the Adriatic. The dense nature of this stone resists water, thus making a primitive but effective damp course. But when flooding occurs, the salt water from the lagoon enters the brickwork *above* the damp course and is carried by capillary action as high as 10 to 15 feet.

Salt water alone would be destructive enough, but the lagoon water is polluted with discharges from Porto Marghera—iron, phenols, cyanides, sulphur, salts, chlorine, naphtha, and detergent solvents. Although the brickwork appears to dry out, it remains impregnated with salt and chemicals, ready to reabsorb moisture from the humid atmosphere. Constantly damp, the brickwork turns to pulp, the stucco falls off, the ends of floor timbers and of iron tie rods are exposed to the ravages of the atmosphere—and the building is then well on the way to collapse. This deterioration is the most obvious sign of the death of Venice. A tour of any of Venice's smaller canals reveals immediately the decay of the city's buildings; high areas bare of stucco, walls of crumbling brick, ground floor windows boarded up, blocks of stone awry because the wave action of the *vaporetti* has eaten away their mortar, house after house closed and abandoned to its fate.

To be fair, industrial development has not *caused* Venice to sink—that has been happening for a long time. As we have seen, there are two main reasons for this: the level of the Adriatic is rising while at the same time the land mass of which Venice is a part is sinking. No one knows exactly how much Venice sank during its early years. The first attempt to measure this was in 1908, when a committee set up by the city council had datum lines, called 'fixed heads', marked on various buildings to be used as check points to determine their relationship to the level of the sea. But, having made the marks, no one got around to taking the measurements until 1952. They were then continued on a regular basis, with major surveys in 1961 and again in 1969. The results were alarming. Some places in Venice had sunk as much as 7 inches between 1908 and 1961. The subsidence between 1952 and 1969 ranged from about 3 inches in Venice to a maximum of nearly 6 inches at Marghera.

In St Mark's Square the fixed head on the Cathedral shows that it has sunk nearly 5 inches, and the Campanile a record 7¼ inches. In the clock tower the fixed head shows a subsidence of 5 inches. In Campo San Stefano the fixed head attached to the base of the monument to Nicolo Tommaseo registers a subsidence of 5¼ inches. The church of Santa Maria Elisabetta, in the main square of the Lido, has sunk 3¾ inches; and at Rialto, the Ca' Loredan, which houses city council offices, has a fixed head that shows the building is sinking at a rate of 4 inches every 50 years.

Admittedly, compared with other cities in Italy and elsewhere, the subsidence in Venice is not extreme. Ravenna has sunk more than a foot, and Ariano 18¼ inches. Mexico City and Long Beach, California, have subsided a massive 25 feet. But in Venice, because of the city's setting, every fraction of an inch is crucial, and the recorded subsidence, modest compared with elsewhere, has meant that the area of the city covered by an *acqua alta* is now *three times greater* than it was fifty years ago.

This would not have happened on this scale from 'natural' subsidence alone. Porto Marghera speeded Venice's sinking by extracting water for industrial purposes. Some fifty-five wells tap five highly productive underground water sources in the upper 300 yards of sand, silt and clay that make up Venice's subsoil. Pumping started in 1930, and by 1969 consumption reached 360,000 gallons an hour. In that year, the Marghera industrialists agreed to drill no new wells and to keep the consumption rate steady while scientific tests were made to determine whether the wells had, in fact, accelerated the natural subsidence. In 1974, scientists from the IBM centre in Venice, the Italian National Research Council and the University of British Columbia were able to state categorically: 'The rate of development of measured subsidence parallels the history of development of the Marghera well-field ... We believe that there is no doubt that the subsidence is caused by the groundwater withdrawals.'

The Porto Marghera industrialists had agreed to drill no new wells and to keep their consumption constant—but they had not agreed to stop it altogether. So since 1969, despite the scientists' findings, pumping has continued. What effect has this had? The earth underneath Venice compacts or consolidates as the water is taken out of it. There is a limit to this process, but the limit has not yet been reached. If the Marghera pumping had stopped in 1974, when the scientists announced their conclusions, then the subsidence would have been arrested at its present level and there might well have been a modest rebound over the next twenty-five years of perhaps half an inch as the earth recovered. But the pumping did not stop. There was no other source of water sufficient for industry and, as the President of the Industrial Zone succinctly pointed out, 'We can be independent of Venice, but Venice cannot live without us.' So, as pumping continues, a further threequarters of an inch of subsidence can be expected before the consolidation process is complete.

Long-term plans call for the construction of more aqueducts to bring water from the Alps to Marghera, but, even if these are eventually built, they will be too late to prevent the final subsidence occurring. True, some of the water from aqueducts could be used to recharge the depleted wells under Venice. But the scientists say that it is too late for this to make

more than a marginal difference. Although it would increase
the *rate* of rebound, it would not increase the *amount* of
rebound. They conclude that 'unfortunately, 85 per cent of
the Venice subsidence is non-recoverable.'

That it increased the rate at which Venice is sinking is not
the only charge against Porto Marghera. As the port grew,
the lagoon had to be adapted to cope with increased traffic.
The main entrance to the lagoon is Porto di Lido, which is
1,000 yards wide. From there, the Giudecca canal runs immediately in front of St Mark's Square, sufficiently close to
cause concern over what would happen if, say, an unwieldy
petrol tanker went out of control and crashed straight into
the Piazzetta between the waterfront and the Square. (This
is not as unlikely as it may sound. In September 1969, a
tanker did go out of control and such a crash did nearly
occur.)

As tankers increased dramatically in size, the Giudecca
canal could no longer cope and in 1967 a new canal, the
Petroleo, was planned to run from the Malamocco entrance
to Marghera. The industrialists did their best to garner support for this canal by pointing out that it would divert
shipping away from Giudecca and allow it to bypass the
heart of Venice. But the new canal ran into difficulties from
the very start. To begin with, it was so long in the planning
that it was already ten years out of date when the work
finally began.

Objections from environmental groups then grew to such
strength that work on the canal had to stop. With nearly a
mile of the canal still to be dredged to the planned depth of
50 feet, work was abandoned at 40 feet. Even then, when the
first tanker attempted to pass through the canal it was
blocked by hundreds of small boats organized in protest by

Venetian architect, Paolo Rosa Salva. Salva and his supporters say that the dredging of the lagoon has changed its character, and that as a result not only does flooding now occur more often but the ocean swirls in faster, higher, and less predictably than before.

Venetians are not fools, and what has been happening to them and their city has not passed unnoticed. Some have taken a strong and unambiguous stance, such as the industrialists—who liken protests by Salva and his supporters to a mediaeval witch hunt—or Gianfranco Pontel, one of the leaders of the Venetian Social Democratic Party. Pontel was born in the historic centre and lived there for twenty-two years before moving to Mestre to a centrally heated, two-bedroom apartment in a modern block with a lift—'to live in the same sort of place in Venice, I'd need to be the nephew of the Aga Khan.' His views probably sum up those of most of the young Venetians who work in Porto Marghera and live in Mestre:

> We have always maintained that if Venice was not to be turned into a museum—and it should not be—there must be a site for industrial activity, and the fulcrum would be Porto Marghera. Venice was the first commercial port in Europe, and the development of the petro-chemical industry was natural. Now Venice must become the great container port of the Common Market, one of the two great Mediterranean outlets of the Nine, along with Marseilles.

The conservationists' case, at its most basic, is put by the Republican Party's Professor Dalla Volta, who sees Porto Marghera and Mestre as "a cancer" that must be cut out if Venice is to survive.

In between the two extremes are the vast majority of

Venetians, who are not quite certain where they stand because no one has put forward a realistic definition of who, or what, Venice is for. Is it for the workers, who want decent housing and employment nearby, or for the rich who want even better housing and no industry at all? Is it for the developers who would like to convert the *palazzi* into magnificent apartments for the new rich of Europe, thus turning Venice into a seaside St Moritz; or for the political Left, who would like all property in the city to be publicly owned—with the few Venetian gardens, for example, turned into public parks? Is Venice primarily for the thousands of families which have lived there for generations, or should it be further developed for the millions of tourists who visit each year, making Venice more like a European Disneyland?

These matters clearly require political decisions, power and finance beyond Venice's own limited capabilities and have, to date, been tackled by the central authorities in Rome. But the very nature of government in Italy, its inherent instability, its system of political favours, and its crushing bureaucracy, made it unsuitable to handle a problem like Venice, and is the basic reason for its spectacular lack of success.

CHAPTER 5

A Law to Stem the Tide

THE framework for Italian politics is the Constitution of
1 January 1948, introduced after Italy's defeat and Mussolini's
downfall at the end of the Second World War and designed
to prevent the recurrence of a Fascist dictatorship. However,
the Allies did not try to remake the nation's political institutions, as they did in Germany; instead, they attempted to
restore democracy by returning to Parliament the powers
which Mussolini had taken from it. The system itself was
unchanged: the Chamber of Deputies and the Senate were
both elected, both with power to initiate legislation, which
must pass both houses. Nor was the basic body of Italian law
changed, and many of the laws passed during the Fascist
regime remained on the statute books. Indeed, many of the
men who had operated those laws remained in their old jobs.

The one innovation in the 1948 Constitution was a third
tier of government, designed to fit snugly between national
politics in Rome and local politics, and based on a division
of Italy into twenty-one regions. The object of these regional
governments was to make the concentration of power in the
hands of a man like Mussolini much more difficult, but there
were side effects. Previously, power to plan lay solely with
local governments, within broad limits laid down in Rome;
now it had to be shared with the regional governments,

Above In the early eighteenth century Canaletto painted this view of Venice near where a bridge across the Grand Canal and the railway station were later built. A detail of the same view today *(below)* is considerably less inspiring.

During the 1966 floods the Adriatic smashed through Venice's great seawalls and left them in ruins.

As the walls of the city crack and crumble, some canals present a picture of mile after mile of rotting beauty.

A capital on the lower broglio of the Ducal Palace: chemicals in the polluted atmosphere ravage the city's sculpture.

The petro-chemical complex at Porto Marghera, across the causeway from Venice, pours its noxious vapours into the sky.

The authorities fight a
losing battle to save
Venice's architecture.
Beneath one piece of
scaffolding, like this on
St Mark's Cathedral, the
sign reads 'Beware –
Falling Angels'.

It is too late to save the
sculpture's detail on the
exterior of the Scuola di
San Marco: the figures
have already lost a nose
here, a finger there.

which was a mixed blessing. As one commentator concluded:
'At best, regional government can inject a new vigour and
more direct democracy into the machinery of government
. . . At worst it can insert a parasitic layer of maladministra-
tion between the central and local government adding to the
opportunities for *clientelismo*, intrigue and corruption.'
(*Clientelismo* is not unique to Italian politics; in America it
would be called log-rolling; in Britain it might be summed
up as 'you scratch my back and I'll scratch yours'.) The
advent of regional government added a new factor to a
political system already painfully complicated.

Put at its simplest, any law in Italy has first to pass both
houses of Parliament. But this does not automatically bring
it into effect, because in Italy a law is not really a law but
more a general guide to Parliament's intentions. The next
step is for the actual manner in which the law will be operated to be established in two documents, *decreti delegati* and
indirizzi, which have to be published before the expiry of
deadlines set in the law itself. Once these are published, the
regional government comes into the picture, since no money
can be spent on implementing a law until its regional implications have been studied and a report made—the *piano
comprensoriale*, or regional plan.

Venice comes within the region of Veneto, so a whole
new level of political power—which is in the hands of men
from towns on such mainland towns as Verona, Padua and
Vicenza—becomes important in determining Venice's future,
because not a penny of Italian government money can be
spent on Venice until these men approve. The opportunities
for bureaucratic delay and *clientelismo* under such a system
help explain the fate of the various laws that Rome has
passed at various times to try to save Venice.

The first, passed in 1937, involved planning controls on Venetian buildings; the second in 1948, was more concerned with the development of the satellite town of Mestre. The scope of the third special law in 1956 was wider, embracing the problems of pollution in the lagoon, and the deterioration of the stone sculpture. The third law was the first to commit the government to spending some money. It amounted to three billion lire (£2 million) and was to be spent entirely improving canals and bridges. It was not a lot of money, but it was a beginning.

The fourth Special Law for Venice was passed in June 1966, only five months before the November floods, after which it was perfectly clear that the government would have to do much, much more. This law had allocated 12 billion lire (£8 million) to be spent on the city and the lagoon, and immediately after the floods the government offered £5½ million more to repair the sea walls. But then, as the extent of Venice's problems emerged, a paralysis seemed to grip the politicians. Three years later, in 1969, Indiro Montanelli, a journalist on the *Corriere della Sera*, took the Mayor of Venice to court, claiming that he and his colleagues should be stripped of their powers because they had spent not a lire of the government grants. But Montanelli's ingenious flourish was overtaken by events: by 1971 the various political parties in Rome had agreed that Venice needed a fifth Special Law, both comprehensive and very expensive.

The essential compromise that preceded the passage of this law was triply difficult to make: there was so much money at stake; the regional government had to be consulted this time; and many conflicting political demands had to be met or appeased. There was outside pressure too, because UNESCO, which had become involved immediately after the floods, had established an office in Rome, and René Maheu, the Director-General, had made it clear they would not move this operation to Venice itself until there was a law to operate. It was two years before the heavily modified proposals passed the Senate, but even that was only the end of the first lap in a race of indeterminate length.

Law number 171 of 16 April 1973 to save Venice was unambiguous. Its first sentence stated that 'Saving Venice and its lagoon is declared a question of the essential national interest.' Here, seven years after the floods, was clear recognition of the importance of Venice's problems. Their urgency was apparently also recognized: the *decreti delegati*, which would deal with fundamental issues like air and water pollution, the restoration of Venetian buildings, and new sanitation schemes, were all scheduled for publication within 120 days of 16 April; within sixty days a list of protected buildings was to be ready, and after a mere thirty days a technical and scientific committee was to be at work. The time scale for the *indirizzi*—which would outline a development plan for the whole of the lagoon—was just three months. The law was littered with short-term deadlines, and if they were met the project to save Venice would be under way by the autumn of 1973.

Even more remarkable was the government's precision about the cost. The total sum was to be 300 billion lire (equivalent to £200 million), and the law contained a strict timetable for its expenditure. Before 1973 was out, 25 billion (£16 million) were to have been spent; in 1974 another 60 billion (£40 million) were to be ploughed into Venice. But the really big spending programmes were to come in 1975,

for which 90 billion (£60 million) were allocated, and 1976
—another 85 billion (£58 million). In the last year of this
dynamic five-year plan the final 40 billion (£27 million)
would flow into the city. It was a detailed and impressive
schedule.

But the law did not just confine itself to a strict timetable.
It also outlined the *way* in which the money was to be spent,
and these job descriptions seemed proof that Italian government had at last grasped the scale of the Venetian problem.
Nothing was overlooked. For a start, 93 billion of the 300
billion lire were committed to regulating the water level of
the lagoon—to building the gates that would prevent the
recurrence of the *acque alte*. This money also had to cover the
cost of dredging the harbours and canals, and, incidentally,
the conservation of state property in the lagoon, of which
there is a good deal. At least it did not have to finance the
planned improvement in dockside facilities in Venice and in
Chioggia, a small port at the southern end of the lagoon;
6 billion had been specially earmarked for that.

The next substantial sum was the 58 billion to be spent by
the regional government for the construction of aqueducts,
which would remove the need for industry to draw water
from under Venice. (Drinking water already came by aque-
duct and pipeline from the mainland to the island, which
is why water is no longer drawn from the well heads that
stand in every *campo*.) This same allocation would also
provide treatment plant to purify polluted water emptying
into the lagoon from the mainland.

The third and largest slice was 100 billion to be spent
mostly in Venice itself (10 per cent was for Chioggia)
restoring decayed housing and building an entirely new
sanitation system, which would reduce the city's dependence

on the tides to get rid of sewage. Another 22 billion were to go to the regional government to spend on improved heating systems and water purifying plants, which would reduce the level of pollution in the air and the water.

The framers of the law also recognized that it was little use having grand plans if there were no experts to do the detailed planning; so 18 billion was allocated to training, and 9 billion more to local and regional governments to cover the cost of the elaborate plans needed to carry out the law's far reaching proposals. It was undoubtedly the most ambitious, comprehensive and generous legislation to be devoted to the crisis of an Italian city—probably of any European city, and perhaps of any city in the world.

But when one talks to Italian politicians to try to discover what went wrong, one senses that they never really shared the sense of elation that was felt at the time by the foreigners who were doing voluntary work for Venice. The politicians, more expert in the ways of Italian administration and the capabilities of Italian bureaucrats, decided that the deadlines were more optimistic than realistic.

Yet the beginning was promising. The law established a Commission to Safeguard Venice, a body with power to cut through the bureaucratic morass; a representative of UNESCO was included on it, thus allowing a non-Italian to have an influence in what diplomats term 'the internal affairs of a sovereign state'. The UNESCO representative was only one of twenty members and could always be outvoted, but at least he was there, a foreign body in the body politic.

The Commission chairman was to be the president of the regional government, and the representatives of the three levels of government, national, regional and local, made up a substantial majority. The rest were technical specialists, a hydrologist, an engineer and a doctor. In his report to a UNESCO conference held in July 1974, René Maheu was able to announce that he personally had attended the first meeting of the Committee on 20 June 1973, barely two months after the passage of the law.

That was the end of Maheu's good news. A technical and scientific committee was proposed by the law as a method of involving experts who had not found a place on the Commission. This was to be set up by the Ministry of Public Works, but Maheu reported sadly that fifteen months after the passage of the law, no technical and scientific committee existed. (One was created much later.)

The *decreti delegati*, filling out vital sections of the law, had all been scheduled for publication 120 days after the passage of the law, on 11 August 1973. It is, perhaps, unrealistic to expect decrees like this to be published at the height of a Roman summer, but the first of the three that were called for was not published until 13 December, and then it contained some appalling omissions. The next did not come out until 1 February of the following year, and the third had still not come out by the summer of 1974, at the time of the UNESCO review.

But the most serious delay of all was that of the *indirizzi*, giving the outlines of general plans for the redevelopment of Venice and the lagoon, and the statement of the principles on which Venice was to be saved. Behind that bland and harmless sounding prospectus lay a political struggle of will and ideology which still threatens to make the law to save Venice redundant by using its own provisions to quicken rather than prevent its destruction.

The *indirizzi* gave rise to a further confusion, which is easier to sort out if one remembers Catch 22, the formula invented by Joseph Heller to demonstrate the victory of bureaucracy over reason. As the months passed after April 1973, there was a growing clamour about the absence of any cash in Venice. When was it going to arrive? Was it a figment of the imagination, or did it really exist? The answer was that the money was there, and could be spent if the *indirizzi* gave guidelines for spending it; but there were no *indirizzi*, because no one had been able to decide how the money should be spent.

Instead of three months, as the timetable outlined, it was two years before the *indirizzi* were published, and for much of that period the people who believed Venice must be saved were not arguing about *how* it should be done; instead they were locked in battle with people who did not want it done at all.

The theme of the *indirizzi* debate was, of course, not unique to Venice. It was common to most industrial societies in the 1960s involving, as it did, the conflict between rising social and economic expectations and the desire to retain as much physical evidence of the past as possible. So the battle was joined between, on one side, the economic expansionists who believed that the best way to save Venice was by development in the third industrial zone across the lagoon in Marghera, and, on the other, the conservationists who asserted that this was the certain way to destroy Venice.

The battle began immediately after the law was passed in April 1973, and continued during the winter and spring of 1974. By the summer, UNESCO was growing impatient, reflecting the views of all concerned foreigners and the innumerable apolitical Italians who have little sympathy for the Byzantine machinations of the politicians. UNESCO had organized for the end of July a meeting of the International

Consultative Committee to Save Venice (a body composed
of distinguished foreigners and Italians, split roughly 50:50),
and the Italian government, in an attempt to appease the
UNESCO Director-General, René Maheu, promised that an
Under-Secretary of State, Adolfo Sarti, would attend,
bringing the *indirizzi* with him to Venice. And so he did—
but he never took them out of his pocket. The documents
leaned towards the conservationist view, and rejected substantial development of the third zone. The local politicians
told Sarti that it simply would not do, and he took them
back to Rome for further revision, lamely promising Maheu
that a new version would be ready by mid-October. But by
then the Christian Democrat government in Rome had
fallen, and Sarti had fallen with it.

When the government re-formed it was without the
Socialist parties of the Left. The Christian Democrats
gambled, and made an alliance with the Republicans. The
coalition was, frankly, expected to have an even shorter life
that most of its predecessors, but the winter passed, and then
the spring, and the economic crisis which had brought the
nation to the brink of bankruptcy in the early summer of
1974 receded. Headed by Aldo Moro, the government
survived, and began to win grudging respect. But for Venice
the significance of the new administration was that it shifted
power away from the industrial developers. The Republicans
are the party most enthusiastic about saving Venice, and
three of its leading figures held the three cabinet posts that
are most vital to the future of Venice—Finance, Public
Works and Fine Arts.

It was, therefore, extremely confusing when the new
draft *indirizzi* which began circulating in Rome in January
1975, were seen to allow extensive development in the third

zone, especially as the *indirizzi* were promised for publication
in April, thus allowing little time for amendment. But by
now there was such impatience that it seemed almost better
to have bad *indirizzi* than none at all. It looked then as though
the government might fall again, creating further delay, but
it limped on and, finally, the deadline was met. Just before
Easter the first copies of the fourteen-page typed document
containing the *indirizzi* reached Venice. Shortly after Easter,
its contents were revealed by the Minister of Public Works,
Pietro Bucalossi. After two years of haggling the outcome
was, unsurprisingly, a compromise. The Left was quietened
by a promise that there would be no unemployment in
Mestre; the industrial developers by a promise of some vague
expansion in the third zone; and the conservationists by the
promise that there would not be too much of it.

At least development in the third zone appeared to be
limited to a container port. The rest, the *indirizzi* announced,
would be allowed to slip back into its natural state. The
existing canal would be deepened to allow larger ships into
Porto Marghera, but the oil port that had already been built
at the tip of the third zone to cater for 250,000 ton tankers
was to be dismantled and moved outside the lagoon. In
future the oil would be piped ashore to the chemical complex. The 42,000 jobs in Porto Marghera were to be protected, making any radical change in the status quo impossible
—which was the most significant conclusion of the *indirizzi*.
However, there were other factors that would loom large
later on: for example, the *indirizzi* ordered that an international competition be held to decide the best way of
closing the lagoon entrances to the *acque alte*, insisted that the
sea walls be strengthened, and demanded stricter pollution
controls. There were also plans for more social services, more

conservation and leisure areas in the lagoon, and for new housing in Venice itself.

The *indirizzi* were thought a cause for considerable congratulation among the people who wished Venice well; so conditioned were they to bad news that it was considered good news that Venice had at least been saved from a rapid death, from being suffocated by unrestrained economic development. Luigi Scano, one of two Republicans on the Venice city council, a thickly-bearded, dark-complexioned man with a fine Venetian face, argued afterwards that the guidelines had been fixed for good. 'It was a compromise, but a very satisfactory one; a political victory for us,' he commented. But nothing is that certain in Venice.

Only days after publication of the *indirizzi*, the director of the Port Authority, General Stochetti, seemed to have an interpretation of them which was radically different from Luigi Scano's. Scano believed that only 400 of the 1,200 hectares reclaimed from the lagoon in the third zone could be used for industry. But Stochetti's plump finger covered twice that amount when he pointed to the area he proposed to develop. Further, the *indirizzi* implied that only container traffic would be allowed in the new port, but the director was already talking about new factories which would, for instance, assemble foreign cars whose parts had been imported separately. His aide, the Social Democrat politician, Gianfranco Pontel, was blunt about it. 'Four hundred hectares are not enough,' he said. It began to look suspiciously as though the Republicans had won a round, but not the fight. Like other victories claimed at other times in Venice, it was possible that, like the city itself seems on a hot, hazy day, the Law to Save Venice was just an illusion, a marvellous dream.

CHAPTER 6

The Loan that Never Was

THE Save Venice law put the cost of the operation at 300 billion lire, and there was much speculation as to how this would be raised. The answer appeared to have arrived on 26 September 1973, when the Italian government issued a loan contract as the first step towards finding the money.

The front cover of the contract is headed by the name Consorzio di Credito per le Opere Publiche, an organization known more conveniently as Crediop, which was set up by the Italian government to raise money nationally and internationally for public spending. The sum came next, and since it was being raised on the Eurodollar market it was expressed as $500 million. (The exchange rates that autumn were convenient, since that converted into 300 billion lire or £200 million.) Then came the title: 'A pre-financing loan agreement in connection with the preservation project of the city of Venice.'

Next came the names of the banks that were going to lend the money. First was the Chase Manhattan of New York City, David Rockefeller's bank, a good start; it was followed by the Bank of Tokyo, then Security Pacific of San Francisco and the European Banking Company. Finally, came the list of merchant banks which would manage the loan for Crediop, persuading the borrowers to lend at the rate of

interest being offered. They were three of the most famous
merchant banks in the western world: Lehman Brothers and
Kuhn Loeb, both of Wall Street, and N. M. Rothschild, of
the City of London.

At that time, the loan was one of the three or four largest
ever raised on the Eurodollar market, and was mentioned in
the *Financial Times* in London. Its correspondent in Rome
reported on 24 September:

> Despite earlier denials, the Italian Credit Institute,
> Crediop, has stated that the $500 million loan now being
> negotiated with a consortium led by Lehman Brothers,
> will be used at least partially to finance the restoration of
> Venice. This agreement is due to be signed in London this
> week. Crediop stated that their negotiations with Lehman
> had been going on for a year or so, originally on the basis
> of a long-term 15 to 20 year bond issue. But due to
> slowness at the Italian end in preparing the planning and
> other work to be financed at Venice, Crediop decided to
> go ahead with a loan on a relatively short six year basis
> instead.

The phrase 'despite earlier denials' was confusing. Had
anyone denied that the loan was for Venice? The Italian
government had always said that it would go to international
money markets to raise the money to save Venice, and, in
fact, it had been widely believed that UNESCO would lend its
prestige to a bond issue, to be taken up by individuals who
loved Venice, and concerned corporations. There had
actually been an unsuccessful attempt to persuade the
American tax authorities to give Venice charitable status,
which would have made the bond issue tax exempt and
particularly attractive to investors. And there had even been

a false start in 1971 when the Prime Minister, Emilio Colombo, announced that the government had already raised a 250 billion lire loan for Venice at favourable rates of interest.

It was, unfortunately, an example of the trouble some politicians have in distinguishing fact from intention. Prime Minister Colombo stated that the intention of his government was 'To bring the problem of Venice out of the shadows where it seems to have remained grounded until now, and set it on the way to a solution in line with Venetian, Italian, and international expectations.' The only thing raised in 1971 was expectations. The 250 billion lire loan was a myth.

But when negotiations for a loan did begin late in 1972, as the debate over the Save Venice legislation was reaching its climax in the Italian Parliament, the idea of a 'Venice loan' had important American allies. George Ball, who had held posts at the State Department in Washington in more administrations than most people could remember, was, among other things, a partner in Lehman Brothers. He was keen to help, and with his wide knowledge of the banking business, he was in an excellent position to do so. He did not mastermind the negotiations for the loan, but always helped them along when he could. His aide at Lehman Brothers remembers the period well. 'The transaction was always referred to in the office as "the Venice loan",' she says.

The name of Venice was obviously important. At Kuhn Loeb's London office a partner remembers that Venice's name gave the loan a particular advantage. 'It persuaded certain banks to subscribe when they might otherwise have said: "We've got too damn much Italian paper on our hands at the moment."' Jacob Rothschild, one of the senior partners in N. M. Rothschild, was keen that his bank should be involved. It was assumed that the American banks lending the money would not have put so much if Venice had not been involved, 'but the prestige was felt at the level of the managers too'.

There was also a cash value to the prestige, because the rates at which the loan was offered were not very generous. Rates on Eurodollar loans like this are calculated by adding a premium onto the prevailing market rate. In this case Crediop offered a premium of five-eighths of one per cent, which Rothschild's described as 'poor'. But the Chase Manhattan Bank were nonetheless willing to stump up around $100 million, so the Venice link *must* have been a factor. In the end, everyone seemed pleased: Crediop had a great deal of money reasonably cheaply, and the banking community felt it had done something useful for Venice.

The money had been raised so effortlessly that within weeks the government was already being asked when they proposed to start spending it. But their response was very strange indeed. 'Spending what?' came the reply. Just how the plot began to thicken was described in two contemporary reports in the *Guardian* from its man in Rome, George Armstrong. The first on 30 November read:

The battle against time to save Venice from its many ailments—a battle which the entire world thought had begun in earnest earlier this year after long delaying scrimmages in the Italian Parliament—has not begun at all. The initial cost of the operation to rescue the city from certain death, about £200 millions, had been collected, we were told, through an international loan. The man who took credit for this was Signor Mario Ferrari Aggradi, the former Minister of Public Works. In fact, the story went, the loan had been oversubscribed by a group of foreign banks and philanthropic organizations. The truth was admitted last night in the Chamber of Deputies in response to a question put to the Under Secretary for Public Works, Signor G. A. Arnoud: 'The international loan under the patronage of UNESCO was never sought,' he said, 'and therefore the money was never collected.'

This was a bizarre statement. Certainly the 1971 loan, the one which was to have been under UNESCO's patronage, was never sought, and, therefore never raised. But that loan was not the subject of the question. It was the loan of 26 September 1973 that aroused the Deputy's curiosity. Signor Arnoud—deliberately or inadvertently—had only added to the confusion. The story could hardly end there, however, and, sure enough, within two weeks Armstrong wrote from Rome again:

The mystery of the missing £200 million which had been promised by foreign banks in 1971 to preserve the sinking city of Venice grows deeper. The official word from the Treasury Minister, Signor La Malfa, is not to worry. The Italian state will fulfil its pledge and thus, incidentally, obey a law passed last April, and the money will be forthcoming. Or, in another interpretation of La Malfa's cryptic statement, the £200 millions is already in the Bank of Italy, and Venice will not be forsaken. The fact is that Italy *did* float a loan in London on 26 September for the same amount as authorized by the special loan. The beneficiary of that loan is now known. Signor Ferrari Aggradi, who when he was Treasury Minister, promoted a law authorizing the international loan, has said in an interview 'the least we can expect is that this matter be cleared up' and that meanwhile, as to the whereabouts of the £200 millions, 'every inference is possible.' However, the only inference seemingly possible from Signor Ferrari Aggradi's words is that the money arranged for the Venice loan has been disbursed elsewhere.

That was the conclusion drawn by at least some of the representatives of the private organizations for helping Venice who knew of the September loan and had been excited by it. When they met in Venice, shortly before Christmas 1973, La Malfa himself flew from Rome to soothe them, and, according to the correspondent of *The Times* of London, he succeeded: 'The Italian government has managed to reassure a group of organizers of international support for the protection of Venice that the £200 million promised by special law for the city's safeguarding is available whatever rumour—and even some ministers—may have suggested to the contrary.'

But this reassurance had not lessened the confusion; if anything, the failure of the fund representatives to discover anything about the whereabouts of the September loan only added to it. The trouble was not that bankers and government departments were speaking with forked tongues, but that they were speaking a different language and had different priorities from the laymen whose sole concern in all this was to see that Venice was saved.

To begin to understand what was going on that winter of 1973–74 it was necessary to refine government and banking jargon down to the simplest level. In January 1974 a series of blunt questions which we put to the bankers elicited this disappointing conclusion: no matter what laymen might have thought about the Venice loan, the bankers knew all along that all the money would not go to Venice.

At Rothschild's, where the senior partner, Edmund de Rothschild, still hoped that their involvement might help Venice, it was always understood that the loan was "pre-financing", or a step *towards* finding all the money for Venice. 'There is no point in borrowing money unless you are going to spend it straight away,' they added professionally. (And, as we have seen, no money could be spent because there was no blueprint for spending it.) Rothschild's understanding was shared at Kuhn Loeb: only *some* of the money would be spent on Venice. 'At the time this loan was put together we certainly genuinely felt that *part* of the sum was intended for the preservation of Venice.' At Lehman Brothers, where the loan had been put together, the assumptions were the same. And at the Chase Manhattan, they were certain that some of the money had already arrived in Venice. The manager of the Italian section of the International Banking Department in New York, Dominic Scaglione, was immensely irritated at suggestions that all might not be well with the loan. 'The suggestion that it has not arrived is a lot of bunk,' he said.

How much, then, of the 'Venice Loan' should be spent on Venice if the Venice lover was not to suspect it had been fixed? There was no agreement about the amount, though at Rothschild's they thought that it might be the sum that the Save Venice law had stated should be spent in 1973. This was not large, amounting to 25 billion lire, or 8 per cent of the 300 billion lire that was supposed to be spent eventually. But it would meet the expectations of the bankers: some money would be spent immediately, and it satisfied the definition on the cover of the loan—it was pre-financing for the Save Venice law.

Clearly the managers at Rothschild's and Kuhn Loeb felt they had done quite enough for Venice by January 1974 to justify some public relations advertising in *The Times*, whose salesmen were asking them to buy space in a special supplement the newspaper was preparing about Venice. Their advertisements were intended to place their pride at the Venice connection on the public record, and they appeared on 2 February 1974.

Kuhn Loeb's was simply its name in a single line of dignified type surrounded by a large white space. Rothschild's consisted of its name and address underneath the significant headline: VENICE PRESERVED. Sandwiched between them was a smaller advertisement paid for by the Italian government. It was a dry history, in small print, of the development of legislation to help Venice from 1937 to the present. It was not advertising copy aimed at a mass audience, which is why many readers would have missed the vital last paragraph. This read:

> The total cost to the state amounts to 300 billion lire, to be drawn over five years; the Minister of the Treasury has been authorized to raise the loans from Crediop and the issue of long term Treasury bonds or special certificates of credit. To cover the costs relative to the year 1973, equal to 25 billion lire, the Minister of the Treasury has already raised a loan with Crediop. The finance for this was raised by Crediop on the [Italian] domestic market, which at the time of the operation—December 1973—offered more attractive terms than those available on the international market.

There was not even a mention of the September loan, which meant that even the limited expectations of the international bankers were to be dashed as well. The message of the advertisement was clear. *None* of the money raised that September by the 'Venice loan' was to be spent in Venice. And to add insult to injury, none of the money raised in Italy had been spent there either.

It seemed like a good time to go to Rome to see if the facts were any less hard to find on the spot. We made appointments with senior men in the Ministry of Public Works and Crediop, but the truth remained elusive, partly because the Italian bureaucracy ignored one of the basic laws of public relations, which is to make sure that everyone tells the same story.

One explanation of the affair came from the Public Works Ministry's Director-General, Dr Michele Martuscelli, the civil servant in charge of implementing the April legislation. He explained that in his opinion there was nothing to be confused about. Had or had not the loan been raised, at least partly, for Venice? 'There was a mistake here,' he replied. 'This money is now destined for other purposes. Originally, it was destined for Venice, but this was abandoned; other channels were created for guaranteeing the finance to meet the Venice law.' The mildest suggestion that, according to the description of the loan, some of the money ought to have been spent in Venice drew only scorn from Dr Martuscelli. 'If we had the money, we would just have had to put it away in a drawer because we were not ready to spend it then.' To terminate discussion on the subject he concluded: 'We realize there is concern abroad, but we have made it clear that there is nothing to worry about.'

Dr Corrado Conti, legal director of Crediop, had a different version of events. He said straight out that it was quite wrong to believe that the money had *ever* been intended for Venice. 'We couldn't be sure that raising money on the Eurodollar market would be quite so easy later in 1973, or early in 1974, so we took the opportunity of raising quite substantial amounts of funds at that time.' Dr Conti then stated quite specifically: 'We did not use the special law for Venice. We borrowed at that time under our own name, without any link to the special law. The law has not been used to raise the money. It was clear that the financing was for our general needs.'

It was not clear at all, not to Lehman Brothers, Rothschild's, Kuhn Loeb, the Chase Manhattan, the Bank of Tokyo, Security Pacific, UNESCO, the Rome correspondent of the *Financial Times* (who had reported Crediop's intentions the previous September), nor to Dr Martuscelli. But that did not worry Dr Conti, who went on to claim that the unusually good interest rate had 'nothing to do with the attachment of the loan's name to Venice.' But there had been a misunderstanding over this surely? 'It is not our fault,' he replied, 'I don't think that Crediop misled the managers of the loan. If there is any confusion it is between the managers and the lending banks.' Which, considering the enthusiasm of the merchant bankers, seems a little hard on them.

In fact, it seems to be much worse than that. To anyone not versed in the practices and the principles of international money markets, it seems a very curious way indeed of raising money. After all, the managers and the lenders were led to believe that at least some of the money would go to Venice, and Crediop, in September, admitted as much; but when the money was received it was diverted elsewhere. Although not false pretences, it was at least breach of promise.

But the relationship between institutional borrowers and

lenders, big banks and big governments, is different from the relationship between individuals. Behaviour can be un-gentlemanly, but that does not make it illegal, so that when they became aware of what had happened, the banks were annoyed, but no more. 'It isn't the first time they've pulled this trick,' said one of the managers. But their reaction was muted for two reasons. When they looked at their contracts they would see that there was no mention of Venice in the legally binding part of the document—a point which was made very firmly in Rome whenever the issue was raised. The second, and best reason, was that what banks care most of all about is getting interest on their money, and eventually the capital itself, and there was never the slightest suggestion that Italy would default on the loan.

So why did Crediop bother with the deception? The reason is to be found in Dr Conti's explanation: that the loan was for general needs.During 1973 Italy was running a heavy balance of payments deficit, and government expenditure was rising fast. A 300 billion lire loan reduced the deficit and government spending at a stroke. This kind of transaction took place with increasingly regularity as economies like Britain's and even France's staggered under the ballooning inflation created by high wages and oil prices. That, in terms of government finance, was a perfectly satisfactory explanation: the economic managers in the Treasury were, no doubt, quite pleased. It was only in terms of saving Venice that the explanation left so much to be desired, because it showed what a low priority the city would have during a severe and prolonged economic crisis.

The effect of all this was not so much to call into question the competence of the Italian authorities; of course they could not keep the 300 billion lire tucked away in a drawer waiting for the detailed plans on which it would be spent. But the effect was no less serious because it called into question their credibility and their motives, and this credibility continued to deteriorate as various arms of the government continued to offer different versions of the original untruth. As late as January 1975, one of the most vociferous of the private fund raisers, the American Colonel James Gray, reported unequivocally in a newsletter to his subscribers: 'You may be comforted to learn that the Italian government has torpedoed baseless reports about misappropriation of funds earmarked for Venice. In a mid-December letter to the *New York Times*, the Italian Credit Consortium for Public Works politely termed such reports "in error", adding that the funds (approximately $550 million) are in a special deposit account as certified by public records.' Maybe some money was in a special deposit account, but not $550 million, for the convincing reason that no government puts that much money in a drawer. The 300 billion exists only on paper, in an annual list of funds appropriated but not spent which is issued each year by the Italian Parliament, and called the *residuo passivi.*

The money still had to be raised, and the confusion over the first 'Venice loan' was not going to help the managers place any further loans. Lehman Brothers were categorical about that. 'If none of the money from the September loan reached Venice, it is going to be much more difficult next time,' they said.

But the most damning thing of all was that none of the reassurances offered by the Italian government could be tested. The reason many laymen would go on believing that the loan had been fiddled, filched, or diverted was that no money arrived in Venice at all. The 25 billion raised in

Rome in 1973 stayed there that year, the next year and the year after. The 60 billion lire that should have been spent in 1974 never arrived.

Some of the 80 billion lire that should have been spent in 1975 arrived, but there are arguments about how much—or how little—and about what happened to it. Not until substantial sums of money did arrive would the cynicism which informed so much opinion about the Italian government be dispelled. And even if some of it did reach Venice, it would be worth, after inflation, at least 50 per cent less than it was when it was voted in the spring of 1973—in hard figures, 450 billion lire would be needed instead of 300 billion lire.

The story of the Venice loan was bizarre enough to produce some inspired cynicism. Bernard Levin, writing in *The Times*, had an unmistakably original solution. He proposed that an international consortium of shady financiers be brought together to launch a Venice bribe:

A gigantic, monumental bribe on an unprecedented scale; we must get so much money in the kitty that we can make it worth the while of absolutely everybody concerned to help rather than hinder with the precious work . . . We will seek out the interested parties and simply give them, if necessary in used 1,000 lire notes, *enormous* sums of money. We shall need, of course, the cooperation of the Venetian authorities; let us find two or three elected officials in key situations, and—perhaps over a cup of coffee in the Campo San Stefano—slip them the necessary; and when Venice itself is tied up we must move to Rome. Here the politicians and civil servants will no doubt come much more expensive; such considerations must not be allowed to deter us—nor will they, for remember, we aim to raise so colossal a sum that everybody involved can be amply provided for at the going rates.

Criticism of the loan affair deeply hurt some Italian politicians, and Levin's proposal that a Venice bribe be raised was taken seriously, and caused special offence. 'How can anyone think that about us?' asked one Roman politician, who had done much to steer the Special Law through the Italian Parliament.

The fact is that politics in Italy *are* different, and politics in Venice, as we shall see, are unusual even by Italian standards.

CHAPTER 7

A Tragedy within a Farce

At the end of the eighteenth century the Venetian play-wright Carlo Gozzi had a few words to say about Venetian lawyers. In Venice lawyers and politicians are entirely inter-changeable, so what Gozzi wrote is particularly relevant to any understanding of its politics both then and today.

Inveterate abuses, introduced in the remote past, and complicated by the ingenuity of lawyers through succes-sive generations (most of them men with subtle brains, some of them devoid of moral rectitude), have been built into a system of pleading as false as it is firmly grounded and imbued with ineradicable insincerity. The system consists for the most part of quibbling on side issues, throwing dust in the eyes of judges, cavilling, misrepre-senting, taking advantage of technical errors, doing every-thing, in short, to gain a cause by indirect means. And from this false system neither honourable nor dishonour-able advocates are able to depart.

The successors to these ancient politicians meet now in one of the most striking town halls anywhere; with the mildly embarrassing title of Palazzo Farsetti, it was built in the twelfth century on the Grand Canal, not far from the Rialto Bridge. It is a come-down from the Ducal Palace from which

Venice was governed until 1826, but compared to the council chambers in similarly sized cities like Stoke-on-Trent or Memphis, Tennessee, it is very grand indeed.

The council chamber is in the long room on the first floor that runs from the front to the back of all unconverted Venetian *palazzi*, and has a painted ceiling which arouses some enthusiasm among art historians. Beneath it the councillors sit on benches which look like the misericords in a church, uncomfortable enough to keep them from dozing during the lengthy proceedings. The public stand around on the hard marble floor at the end of the room, separated from the councillors by well-groomed young policemen who make cynical observations to spectators and council members alike. They appear to know more than is good for them.

The public part of the room is dominated by a large painting in Venetian style, done by a follower of Tintoretto or Veronese, which can, during the long wait for something to happen, become a metaphor of Venetian government. Down in the left hand corner is a child who could presumably be the infant Jesus, but much more central is the food and wine being served to the man of substance sitting at the nearby table; on the right a lady lies comfortably in bed being cosseted. Behind the infant, a woman offers it one naked breast, while the other is being lecherously fondled. The painting is not what you expect to find in a council chamber, but it is not unsuitable, suggesting as strongly as it does a combination of greed, venality and comfort. For the men who have worked in this room, the struggle between the religious preoccupations of faith, hope and charity and the materialistic ones of power and money has usually been a one-sided contest.

The key to understanding Italian politics lies in the West's determination at the end of the Second World War to prevent the election of a Communist government. The Allies chose the Christian Democrats to be the instrument to keep the Communists out. But the Christian Democrats could govern only with the aid of other parties. The result has been a series of shaky alliances that have survived only as long as basic differences in policy could be compromised. When this was no longer possible the government would fall and another coalition would emerge. In this respect Venice has not been very different from the nation as a whole in the broad complexion of its government. There was one Communist-dominated administration briefly after the war, but it fell when the Socialist Party split. The Christian Democrats took over, and through a series of coalitions with Socialists or Social Democrats, or both, stayed in power un-interruptedly until 1975, for thirty crucial years of Venetian history. During that generation the Christian Democrats were able to seed their supporters in the bureaucracy, and watch their influence steadily grow. But despite the power they were able to wield, they never won a simple majority of votes in local elections. At best they could count on 40 per cent of the electorate—a class group made up of lawyers, businessmen, *petit bourgeois* like shopkeepers, of whom there are many, and women who, for years after the war, fled into the Christian Democrat embrace through fear of Commu-nism. It was a conservative alliance, and could never be expected to initiate radical changes in the pattern of Venetian life.

By the 1970s, when it was no longer able to rely on a solid female vote and its inertia had begun to alienate the new wave of Italian business technocrats, who were appalled by the inefficiency of it all, a section of the party moved left from the centre. Venice's Mayor in the early 1970s, Giorgio Longo, was a member of this group, but it turned out to be no more efficient because the left-wing Christian Democrats alienated the entrenched conservatives in the party on the mainland, and had less influence with the government in Rome.

The most substantial opposition to Longo came from the Communist Party, which had consistently polled about a quarter of the votes in Venice. The party is run from one of the dowdiest buildings on the Grand Canal, reached through a maze of alleys behind an old church which has been converted into a practice hall for the local band. The party was led by Gianni Pellicani, a parliamentarian in Rome, a crisp figure with flashing white cuffs and fashionable clothes which would be regarded as dangerously revisionist by the British Communist Party or the American Left.

The Party's support is from traditional areas—the gondoliers, for example, who are militant trade unionists. In the style of Italian Communism, its policies have been quite unrevolutionary, concentrating on better housing and jobs. It is the kind of low-key, left-wing programme argued in tones of quiet respectability by men like Pellicani that has increasingly seduced the Italian electorate. If Pellicani ever mentions the word revolution, it is certainly not at a public meeting.

The Socialist Party cuts more dash, and wins fewer votes. It is led by men-about-Venice like Giuseppe Mazzariol, an art historian, and Gianni de Michelis, described some years ago as 'Venice's Kennedy', an unselfconscious figure who declaims about the rights of man and the wickedness of the foreign press as he sits comfortably sipping his drink in

fashionable Florian's. The Socialist Party is also split into left
and right: the left wants development in Venice, the right
does not. Mazzariol is right-wing, de Michelis left, although
Mazzariol would argue that *he* was the radical.

The Social Democrats consistently joined a succession of
coalitions, in Rome as well as Venice, to try to inject some
non-Marxist socialism into Christian Democracy, but as
time went by they became increasingly preoccupied with
anti-Communism; the result was a sterility which could be
observed as clearly in Venice as elsewhere. Gianfranco Pontel
talks about Venice in terms of the regeneration of the
managerial class, claiming that the party appeals to white
collar workers, and since they continue to poll just under
10 per cent of the vote it would be cavalier to dismiss them
too easily.

Supporters of the last major party, the Republicans, tend
to belong to the middle, or even the small upper class. The
Party has become one of brave, but lost, causes, and is rarely
heard in the council chamber, because there are so few voices
to speak for it. But Italian politics can shift suddenly, and
even the smallest parties can snatch the power to do something they care about; the Republicans have been fortunate
that way. Of all Italian parties, they are the most committed
to saving Venice—they are against industrial development of
almost any kind, for the immediate control of the lagoon
entrances, and for the rigorous implementation of anti-
pollution laws. It is, in Venetian terms, the straight liberal
ticket, perfect in every way, except, maybe, in its political
practicability.

The Republicans' origin excluded them from the possibility of power for a generation. They had splintered off
from another party of relative insignificance—the Liberal

Party, which had led the right-wing democratic opposition
to Mussolini, and which remained right-wing long after
Il Duce had ceased to provide them with an adequate reason
for their existence. But one of the more attractive qualities
of the Republicans is their optimism—the belief that if they
say something often enough it might happen. In the autumn
of 1974 it did. The Socialists and Social Democrats left the
national coalition, and the Republicans took their place. To
widespread astonishment, not least among its own members,
the new coalition survived, and—as we have seen—the three
cabinet posts of most significance to Venice were all held by
Republicans. (It was their finest hour, because when Venetian
voters were given a chance to reward the Republicans in the
1975 council elections, they did not do so.)

The Fascists are not as important in Venice as they are in
nearby mainland towns like Padua, Verona and Mantua. The
Maoists and extreme leftists are small in numbers too,
perhaps because there are so few Fascists to react to. Venetian
politics are unsympathetic to political extremism, which is
the only benefit its inertia brings.

So the politicians in Venice line up like this. Those in
favour of conservation are the Republicans, the de Martino
Socialists and the Communists. Those who favour 'free
development' are the Christian Democrats – including their
left-wing – the Social Democrats, the de Michelis Socialists
and the Liberals. This is not a line-up based on *national*
political parties and many Venetians would disagree with
this division, but it is a useful basic guide to political attitudes
on the issue which divided Venice more than any other in the
first five years of the 1970s—the dispute over the *piani
particolareggiati*, the detailed town plans. The plans mattered,
not because they brought these politicians and their

parties to life but because they were vital to the fate of Venice.

Town planning is comparatively new in Italy. It got under way during the war, when Mussolini's administration ordered, quite sensibly, that detailed city planning could not take place without considering its effects on the broader environment. Planning was, therefore, to be done on two levels. The first was the general plan, or *piano regolatore generale*, embracing broad areas of policy like transport, communications and industry. Complementary to the general plan were to be the *piani particolareggiati*, which set out in street-by-street detail the plans for the city itself.

After the war it was realized that the bureaucratic drudgery involved in carrying through all the requirements of the planning laws was stifling development in even the most capably run Italian cities, and since many had suffered war damage and needed to hurry plans through, the government passed amending legislation in 1952 allowing city administrations to cut a few corners—making it easier, among other things, for officials to slip plans past an unsuspecting public.

The complex framework of all this legal regulation is best explained by a young Venetian architect called Ferrucio Ferrante. He points out that the general plan for the Venice region—the *piano regolatore generale*—did not appear until 1962, and was not much use to Venice because on all the planning maps the whole island was left entirely blank. It was supposed to await the detailed plan—a wait that lasted eleven years.

Normally, several extra years would have been allowed for revisions to the detailed plan too, but in 1973 the legal basis for Venice's town planning suddenly shifted. The law to save

Venice, passed in Rome in April 1973, stated that all previous
planning laws in Venice would be superseded on 1 January
1975. This meant that if the council had not produced its own
detailed plans by then, the power to plan would be taken out
of the council's hands and passed to the Magistrato alle
Acque, an appointee of the Rome government, and, frankly,
no maestro at getting things done. Most significant of all, it
would mean that the 100 billion lire (£66 million) intended
mainly for the restoration of housing in Venice would be
spent by someone other than the council. Faced with the
prospect of surrendering some of their spending power—
and the patronage that goes with it—Venetian politicians
sprang into action. Where, they demanded of Venice's civil
servants, is the detailed plan?

Present day Venetian bureaucracy is simply not geared to
producing crisis solutions at short notice. Venice's government was once so efficient and impartial that it was considered one of the wonders of the world. It still is, but for
other reasons. In Italy itself, it is knowingly and contemptu-
ously described as 'the Naples of the North'. One example
will suffice. The Montedison chemical complex in Porto
Marghera which spewed its fumes into the atmosphere and
its filthy water into the lagoon, agreed under pressure from
the government in the late 1960s, to try to stop this pollution.
The company found ways of purifying the smoke, and built
a pilot water purification scheme to isolate oily sludge and
turn the dirty brown liquid into clean water before returning
it to the lagoon.

By the mid-1970s, Montedison was committed to spend
billions of lire extending the water purification scheme. There
was only one thing which stopped it from actually doing so;

it could not get planning permission. The Montedison man whose job it was to steer the permission through the Venetian bureaucracy was a clinical study in frustration. He described the continual process of rejection with his head in his hands, lifting the former occasionally so he could wring the latter. He outlined the procedure which has broken him.

All plans involving the lagoon, as Montedison's obviously did, had to be agreed by the Magistrato alle Acque, who has to oversee everything from constructing a purification plant costing billions of lire to an outhouse costing thousands. Planning applications like Montedison's also had to go through various sectors of the local government. First there was the registration department, which noted formal receipt of the application. This had taken a month or so. The documents were then passed to another section to determine which of the city's departments would handle the application—a somewhat dubious process since the application would have to go to the architect's department anyway. When it finally got there, none of the civil servants was able to inspect and pass the plans because their training had been in house construction rather than purification plants in chemical factories. Since the plans were not understood they could not be passed, and while they mouldered away, the lagoon remained filthy.

Given this background, no one should have been surprised at the response of Venice's civil servants to the politicians' demands for an immediate and detailed town plan. Yet the plan was presented in such a way that the disastrous consequences of its possible implementation were not immediately apparent. We first heard of the plan in December 1973, when we received two bulky volumes of documentation produced in Venice entitled *Relazione Generale sul Piani Particolareggiati del Centro Storico*. They had come to us, illicitly we learnt, via a contact in Verona. The reason for subterfuge in getting the plan to us soon became apparent. It provided for a radical change in Venice's appearance. The city was to be divided into two zones, Zone A and Zone B. In Zone A, all buildings would be preserved and restored and no new construction would be permitted. In Zone B, the local council would be entitled to approve wholesale redevelopment of substantial areas of Venice, especially around the docks, on the Giudecca, in the dowdy area of Castello around the Arsenale, and in Cannaregio, stretching away behind the railway station.

When we went to Venice the following month, two points about the plan were immediately obvious. The first was that whoever developed Zone B—private developers or the council itself—whole areas would be torn down, as many as 7,000 new rooms could be built, and an irremediable swathe cut through the Venice skyline. The second point was that council officials were extremely nervous about our enquiries. It emerged, for instance, that the plan had been kept so secret that the Superintendent of Monuments, the man employed by the Italian government to safeguard the city's architecture, had to slip around to UNESCO's office to look at a copy it had managed to acquire, because the council had not given him one.

On Sunday, 3 February 1974, we wrote an article which appeared on the front page of the *Sunday Times*, headlined SECRET PLAN FOR VENICE THREATENS CLASSIC SKYLINE. It began:

Venice, slowly sinking into the waters of the Adriatic and ravaged by industrial pollution, is now facing another kind of death. And this time the wound is self-inflicted.

The city fathers have produced a secret plan for Venice's redevelopment which many fear will attract international property speculators and force out thousands of native Venetians. The *Sunday Times* has acquired a copy of the plan. Although copies have been circulating privately in Venice for the past two months, not even those local and international bodies that are trying to save Venice have been given formal notification of the proposals. The plan, foreshadowed by special government legislation in 1973, was expected to give for the first time precise details about how the Venice council proposed restoring and preserving the city as part of the cultural heritage not only of Italy, but of the Western world. But what the plan actually does is to suggest that substantial areas of the city could be pulled down section by section. They could then be redeveloped on the basis of legislation so permissive that it could lead to the complete alteration of the centuries old Venetian skyline.

The article caused a furore. The Mayor, Giorgio Longo, dismissed it as a tissue of lies, and said that he would invite the international press to see for themselves how the plan would work (he never did). The *Gazzettino*, Venice's daily newspaper, devoted a page to refute our accusations. In Britain, the chairman of Venice in Peril, Lord Norwich, appeared on BBC radio to say that he was quite sure the story was not true, though he later recanted. It was perfectly clear that the article had pricked a very sensitive nerve of Venetian politics. Each time we returned to Venice, some politician or other would give a light shake of the head and say that we should not have written the article: it had held back the restoration of the city. It was even included in an official chronology of Venice's problems: '3 Febbraio—Il *Sunday Times* pubblica un articolo di denuncia control il Comune di Venezia in materia di painificazione urbanistica.'

The fact is that a debate over the plan would have taken place anyway, but it was a symptom of the secretive and self-interested way in which Venetian city planning was conducted that the discussion should have been triggered by an article in a foreign newspaper. Once the gory details had been published, the Italian government acted quickly to curb the council's plans. A decree of 28 March 1974, stated that any area containing buildings of merit must be preserved whole. This destroyed much of the original plan. The Giudecca, for instance, most of which had been included in a B Zone, was transformed overnight into a predominantly Zone A area. The council planners had to go back to the drawing board and prepare another set of *piani particolareggiati*, and although Zone B was still there when they appeared, it was considerably smaller and less damaging than it had been in the first edition.

But why had Zone B been there in the first place? The planners had argued that redevelopment would provide Venice with large areas of new housing. This would allow the Christian Democrats to distribute some profitable building contracts, and would enable both them and the Socialists to rehouse some of their supporters. So it won immediate political support. The opposition to the plan was made up of politicians who saw Venice as something more than a pork barrel. Some, like the Socialist art historian Giuseppe Mazzariol, wanted as little development as possible and resources devoted instead to restoring housing in which Venetians now live. This was the attitude struck by the Republicans too, and by the group of foreign volunteer workers, though, as visitors, they are not always the most reliable analysts of Venice's problems. (They have not had to live in a damp ground floor apartment, without a bathroom, with poor schooling for the children, and health services notably worse than those which Italians on the mainland take for granted.)

Another facet of the argument was that if houses were to be restored, the people who lived in them would have to be housed somewhere else while this work was being done. So there then began a search for what became known as *casa di parcheggio*, 'parking houses'. These were not easy to find. There were the naval barracks down by the Arsenale, but the navy did not want to give them up, and the prospect of barrack life was not especially pleasing to Venetians.

The council conducted a survey of empty buildings in Venice, and the Left clearly enjoyed the prospect of commandeering private property for parking houses. The operation was certainly not without political inspiration; the take-over list included the Palazzo Grimani on the Grand Canal, which had been bought as a training centre by Bruno Visentini when he was chairman of Olivetti and before he became Italy's Finance Minister in the summer of 1974. It had been empty, as had the apartments of some rich Europeans who used Venice as a spring and autumn residence.

During this period whenever two property owners met they would soon be swapping horror stories of the casual way in which their apartments had been listed as parking houses. They need not have worried: the law in Italy is deeply biased in favour of the private owner, and the expropriation of private property would certainly not have provided enough parking houses for the radical restoration of Venice that was envisaged. So the planners were stranded in a characteristically Venetian situation: whatever they did would be wrong by the standards of almost everyone involved. It looked as though there would have to be some new housing, more than the hardened preservationists wanted, but less than the ruling coalition had originally conceived. By the end of 1974 there was grudging but general agreement about the need for at least some B-Zones.

While the debate over the detailed plan went on, many a Venetian found himself in a difficult situation. No alterations to Venetian housing could be undertaken without planning permission, but permission could not be granted until the detailed plan had been completed. The impasse was often broken by contractors who put up a dense straw scaffold screen around a house, went ahead with the work and relied on the inability of the bureaucracy to catch up with them soon enough. Their faith was not often misplaced, for Venetian bureaucracy is usually fully occupied trying to solve problems it has itself created. For example, planning the restoration of housing involved two departments of the administration—one involved with the fabric of the house, and the other with the new sewage systems being intoduced. Unfortunately each department started pilot projects in different areas: housing was restored in one area, while the new sewage system was installed somewhere else. The houses restored did not have the new sewage system, so to install it they would have to be restored all over again.

By the end of 1974 the detailed city plan was, after twelve years in the making, still being re-thought after the Zone A –Zone B fiasco. The areas, or compartments, into which the city should have been divided were still without distinct boundaries, and hundreds of specific proposals had been included without any obvious motive. Certainly the Giudecca is short of children's nurseries, but planning for twenty of them sounded like overkill. It is true that the shopping street called the Frezzeria is not easily accessible, but cutting a new street through to it from the main thoroughfare behind the Grand Canal looked like using a sledgehammer to crack a nut. There is, indeed, a shortage of public gardens in Venice, but it seemed unnecessarily insulting to Peggy Guggenheim, who opens her house to tourists twice a week in the summer so they may see her collection of modern art, to expropriate her garden. ('What's she worrying about?' one insensitive politician complained. 'We won't let the dogs piss on the pictures.')

Much of the work on the plan had been done by young architectural students, and it showed. But the main reason for the plan's shortcomings was haste: it all had to be done at the last minute to meet that 1 January 1975 deadline, imposed by Rome along with the threat of transferring spending and planning powers to the Magistrato alle Acque.

It was not enough to have the plan: there had to be a majority for it in the city council chamber too, and the divisions within the ruling coalition made that problematical. There was only one safe way of making sure that the detailed plan passed the council, and that was to persuade the Communist Party not to oppose it. But why should the Communists bail out their opponents?

What happened in Venice in the winter of 1974 was an example of what is called in Italy 'the historic compromise'. The Communists did not much like the plan, but they, like all the other parties, were even less enamoured of the prospect of power passing to the Magistrato alle Acque. So they did not vote against the coalition administration and on 31 December, after years of wrangling, the detailed plan was passed in the council chamber.

Among the politicians this was greeted with varying degrees of congratulation. The de Michelis Socialists were delighted, as were many of the Christian Democrats, though some of their property-owning supporters could hardly have been pleased at some of the more cavalier proposals for the public ownership of parking houses. The Communists shrugged their shoulders and said that it was worthwhile just to get things moving so that some of the money which had been promised to Venice some twenty months earlier might begin to flow in the city. The Republicans were appalled and hoped that the plan could still be sabotaged.

And so it could, for it would be a mistake to believe that the debate over the plan had ended when it had passed the council. There were not only individual objections to particular proposals—750 or so were lodged during the month the plans were on show, including one from Venice in Peril's Sir Ashley Clarke, whose own garden was imperilled by a plan to turn it into a playground for a nursery school. The Republican Party was openly hoping that the whole thing would be overturned by the regional government, which still had to give its approval before the plan took effect.

The term 'regional government' suggests a body foreign to Venice, but its headquarters are down the Grand Canal from the Venice council's Palazzo Farsetti. It meets in a vast room of the Palazzo Balbi, where around the hall there is a frieze representing the triumph of Venice. The figures look very different from the defeated or apparently disinterested men who meet there now. But the regional councillors reflect the conservative inclinations of the mainland, where Christian Democrats regard their colleagues from Venice as dangerous radicals. It would be easy enough to delay work on the detailed city plan if it could be seen to conflict with the earlier general plan for the Veneto region. So throughout the winter and spring of 1975 they just sat on it.

(It was some small comfort to know that even if the regional government had not stopped the detailed plan, building would not necessarily have gone ahead. We were sitting with Gianni de Michelis and listening to him talking about how insensitive foreigners like ourselves have held up the council's plans for new housing for years by complaints and obstruction. 'Well,' we said in conciliatory tones, hoping to make the best of it, 'what sort of plans do you have for the new housing now it looks as though some will be allowed?' 'Oh, we don't have any plans yet,' he replied.)

Meanwhile, UNESCO's Venice office had looked at the new detailed plan and found it wanting. Immediately, a study group led by Leonardo Benevolo, a distinguished Roman academic, was organized: ostensibly to consider the plan; in fact, to rebut it. In the remarkably short period of four months, Benevolo had produced his study, and UNESCO were able to use it as the basis for a conference of international experts specially convened to discuss the matter. Benevolo is a tall, lean, capable architect, full of fine analysis. He is a scientific planner, contemptuous of the politicians' self-absorbed approach to Venice's problems. The first priority, he argued, was to stop emigration from Venice to the mainland, by providing restored housing at low rents, decent schools and hospitals. But that was not enough: the detailed plan lacked any analysis of what Venice contained, and what it was good for. 'Look at the water gates to the houses, all closed,' he said. 'Venice is a city on water, and yet it hardly uses the water. It didn't even invent the *vaporetto*. Venice has become a city without a role, colonised by tourists and by Milanese and Turin industrialists. They use Venetian labour in their Mestre factories but they ignore the place their workers come from.' This analysis is instantly recognizable to any outside observer of Venetian politics, as is his solution: the development of marine industries, especially in the Arsenale, a vast, and now almost completely empty site.

But Benevolo and the international experts could not agree on what should be done about the immediate matter of the detailed plan. The experts studied Benevolo's report and concluded that he had found, on the one hand, that the city council's detailed plan was 'useless' and the division of the city into two zones 'a grave error', but on the other hand that work on the *new* detailed plan should be carried out by the very same city council. They added that 'Benevolo's report makes a severe criticism of, yet at the same time affirms support for, a very powerful organizing body'— which suggests that the experts did not trust the council to do anything about a new detailed plan without making a mess of it.

Italian experts like Benevolo argued that were the council allowed to do nothing itself, this would ensure that nothing at all could be done. They believed that it was better to work with the council, pay the fees of outside experts, and organize special studies at Venice University.

Benevolo had proposed an approach that was as scientific as was possible within the arena of local politics; but, by 1975, cynicism was not confined to outsiders, and ran deep among Venetians themselves. Visitors who inquired were told that Venetians no longer wanted to discuss their problems. However there was one who did—Vladimiro Dorigo, an author, who works for the Biennale. When asked about the future of Venice he responded with a well organized monologue, with small climaxes leading to a grand conclusion suggesting that whatever is proposed will certainly be wrong. It went like this:

What worries me is the fashionable view at the moment—that all Venice's problems will be solved if pollution is eliminated and Venice is returned to a pre-industrial condition. That is a delusion. This is the twentieth century and people can't live in it as though it were the seventeenth century. There are structural problems—engineering problems with scientific solutions—of great complexity, and the real trouble in Venice is that they are being dealt with by politicians and bureaucrats who are not up to it. In Venice these people deal with everything—industry, restoration, the arts—in an amateurish sort of way. Politicians aren't capable of handling the simplest problems of administration because of the way they are selected. They are in power because of party, money, religion, and the ability to keep quiet. The result is the selection of fools instead of technically qualified capable professionals.

The politicians will change, but the property speculators will go on. The tourists will continue to visit here, but the Venetians themselves will become increasingly insensitive to their surroundings. The operations designed to mend the cracks will continue, but they are not enough. Time is limited, and the men who govern Venice seem incapable

CHAPTER 8

A Moral Obligation

THERE *was* one moment when it looked as though saving Venice would not be left to Italian politicians. In November 1966 Venice could have become a great international crusade. One senior member of the Italian Foreign Office, recalling the chaos in the weeks after the great flood, believes that if UNESCO had acted decisively then, and, as the representative of the international community, had insisted on controlling the work in Venice, the Italian government would have agreed, much as the Egyptian government had done when the temples of Abu Simbel had to be saved from the Nile waters building up behind the Aswan High dam.

There was no doubt about the depth of UNESCO's concern. Its Director-General, René Maheu, an austere figure who had previously been headmaster of a French lycée, was an intellectual with a deep love for Venice. As soon as the first estimates of the damage in Venice and Florence were calculated, Maheu cut through the layers of bureaucracy at UNESCO's Paris headquarters, and had an international appeal ready within a month. It was marvellously comprehensive: directed at governments, which were asked to give money, material, manpower and expertise; at museums, libraries, learned institutions, international associations of librarians and archivists; at writers, musicians, artists, critics and historians; and finally, at art galleries, collectors, theatres, and concert halls. All were asked to give what they could to help save a unique city.

But in retrospect UNESCO's appeal does not seem to have been sufficiently directed at the Italian government. It was significant that, before making the appeal, UNESCO had checked with the President of the Italian Council of Ministers, Amintore Fanfani, to make certain it would be diplomatically acceptable. But Maheu had not asked, in return, for guarantees of action; certainly not that UNESCO be allowed to control the undertaking. He no doubt considered it would have been undiplomatic to have done so: nothing perturbs a UN agency more than the suggestion that it is interfering in the internal affairs of a member state, especially a rich, European one.

The opportunity to internationalize the task of saving Venice was lost then in 1966, and René Maheu was to spend the next eight years of his life, until his retirement in 1974, battling against the results of that lost moment. Instead of an international crusade, it became Maheu's personal one, and at the end of his part in it he had few illusions. 'Venice is a problem of one of the most refined cities in the world,' he said. 'I'm afraid that its very refinement makes it less susceptible to change.'

UNESCO opened its own office in Venice in 1973. The Italian government gave it a suite of rooms in the old state apartments of King Victor Emmanuel III, and even though they had not been redecorated since the collapse of the Italian monarchy in 1945, they were still very grand indeed; vast rooms with marble floors and fabric on the walls, and a view over the public gardens behind St Mark's Square. Joseph Martin, a French Canadian, had been personally selected by Maheu to run the place. He had been deputy director of the National Gallery of Canada in Ottawa. He had European languages and North American attitudes, which seemed good qualifications, and he also had the able assistance of Maria Teresa Rubin, whose command of the complexities of Venetian politics was considerable.

Moreover, Martin sat permanently on the Commission to Safeguard Venice, the political body headed by Angelo Tomellieri without whose permission nothing could be done in Venice. It was a high-powered Commission comprising many of the men who controlled the fate of Venice, and to be a member was to have access to the decision-making process. It was, as Italian politicians never failed to point out, a considerable concession to offer membership to a non-Italian representing an international organization.

UNESCO had managed this degree of recognition after years of hard lobbying in Rome, and it was natural enough that an international bureaucracy should see real advantage in being accepted into the previously closed world of a national bureaucracy. And although UNESCO's role eventually turned out to be better on paper than in practice, it did succeed at first in getting things done. The closely typed seventeen-page evaluation of UNESCO's operation, produced by its Paris office in 1973 for the International Consultative Committee, listed some undeniable achievements, like the preparation of the excellent *Rapporto su Venezia* in 1968, which had been the first to bring together the work of various scientific experts in such a concentrated way as to dramatize the city's parlous condition. There were also sections detailing UNESCO's decision to pay for the compiling of the vital list of buildings and

statues that were threatened—something the Superinten-
dencies of architecture and painting had always been too
busy and too undermanned to do themselves.

The document referred, touchingly, to the praise UNESCO
had received from Italian politicians. 'The head and various
members of the government have on many occasions recognized the decisive part that the "moral pressure" of world
opinion and the collaboration of UNESCO have played in the
new political awareness which led to the recent decisions of
the Italian Parliament.' That was in February 1973, when the
Save Venice law was about to go through. UNESCO believed,
then as now, that its passage so soon after a meeting of the
International Consultative Committee was no coincidence.

This belief in the power of moral pressure was to reappear
later in the document, when the authors considered whether
international co-operation was still of any use to Venice.

Firstly, one might observe that the participation of the
international community is a *moral obligation* [UNESCO's
italics]. If Venice really represents, in the eyes of many
men and women, a vital common asset, then they must
share the burden of its preservation . . . An enterprise of
this kind can represent the 'honour of a lifetime' . . . or, on
the other hand, a lost opportunity. Anyone is free, of
course, to leave the task to others, but those with most
pride and greatest wisdom will want to say 'I took part'.

That sounds like the authentic voice of René Maheu, and its
significance is the implication that no matter what happened,
he had no intention of allowing UNESCO to abandon the task.
But eight months later, towards the end of 1973, he was
beginning to have doubts.

In October 1973 the President of Italy, Giovanni Leone,

visited the UNESCO headquarters in Paris, and Maheu made a long speech during which he said: 'I can assure you, Mr President, that [the representative of UNESCO] will assist the competent Italian authorities with all due discretion, but also with the unflagging attention necessarily prompted by devotion to so lofty a cause.' For some months after that, Maheu's acolytes would point to this sentence, which the casual observer might well have missed, whenever anyone asked what UNESCO could do to hurry up the Italian authorities. It was as close as Maheu got to public criticism.

The following winter increased his disappointment. There was no sign that the large sum of money for which UNESCO had so long lobbied in Rome, and which had apparently been raised with such a flourish on the Eurodollar market, was ever going to *reach* Venice, much less be spent. But there was nothing a self-respecting UN agency dared say about a thing like that.

There was also the worrying business about the division of Venice into Zone A and Zone B, which had caused such concern to the UNESCO office in Venice; and there were strong rumours that the *indirizzi*—the regulations governing the working of the Save Venice law—would be drawn so permissively as to allow further massive industrial development across the lagoon in Porto Marghera.

In the spring of 1974 Maheu wrote to the Italian government pointing out that the International Consultative Committee would be meeting in Venice in July, and that he hoped there would be by then news to appease their growing concern at the remarkably casual way in which the whole operation seemed to be conducted. Maheu received a pleasantly polite reply, but nothing happened; and the Director-General finally began to lose his patience. When he

D   97

arrived in Venice for the July meeting he was talking to close colleagues about a dramatic protest against the Italian government's attitude—he would close the Venice office, the great symbol of UNESCO's commitment to the city.

The 1974 meeting of the International Consultative Committee was a three-day affair held in one of the conference rooms at the Cini Foundation on the island of San Giorgio Maggiore. At the back of the room were all the trappings of an international meeting—multi-lingual bureaucrats handing out multi-lingual conference papers, and boxes in which interpreters sent out the message in English, French and Italian. The chairman was René Huyghe, a French Academician and historian. He was flanked by Bruno Visentini, the boss of Olivetti, one of the symbols of Italy's economic recovery; and among other distinguished members were Sir John Pope-Hennessy, the impassive and authoritative then director of the British Museum, a Japanese, who said nothing, but smiled politely and was rumoured to control the spending of immense sums of money; a Brazilian who also said nothing but had no access to a fortune either; and a German, Hans von Herwarth, who had all the confidence of a retired diplomat from one of the world's most powerful nations. Venice itself was represented by Countess Anna Maria Cicogna, quintessentially a figure of the Italian establishment, but aristocratically dismissive of its political section. There were other Italians too—professors of this and that, great men in their fields, so everyone said, and rightly too, though they themselves said little.

The Committee obviously had real pulling power. Seated by Maheu was one of the government's Under Secretaries of State, Adolfo Sarti, who was in Venice for the duration of the meeting. Further along the top table was the Mayor of Venice, Giorgio Longo. The President of the regional government, Angelo Tomellieri, was the only senior man who could not attend, but he had sent along a bright young politician, Marino Cortese.

The first three speakers were all Italian politicians, and when what each said was added up, there was very little ground for optimism among International Consultative Committee members or observers from independent committees, like Sir Ashley Clarke of Britain's Venice in Peril. The Mayor of Venice spoke first, conceding that there could be no more delay in saving Venice, and adding that he hoped that something might get going by the following November. But he reflected the impatience which many Venetian politicians feel towards UNESCO. He was far too polite to echo the assertion of the Socialist, Gianni de Michelis—'UNESCO came on the Venice scene only because it was finished at Abu Simbel, and now it would have us become a cross between a Nubian monument and Disneyland'—but the Mayor certainly appeared to sympathize with this view. He said that Venice could not merely be a monument, that it was a city in which people lived—which sounded unexceptional enough, except that this slogan had become a euphemism for the development of new housing in Venice and more industry in Porto Marghera. Listening to the Mayor, it even seemed possible that Venetians like himself did not really care for the place; clearly they regarded it quite differently from the visitors in the room, who were there because of Venice's art and architecture.

The next speaker was Marino Cortese, the young man from the regional government, who lectured the conference about the real world in which its discussions were taking place. There was, he pointed out, appalling inflation (running then at 20 per cent a year), and governments like his were only just beginning to grasp its implications. For example, the Save Venice law had suggested a sum of 58 billion lire (£38 million) to build the aqueducts that were to bring water from the Alps for industry at Porto Marghera. The regional government had done its sums and decided that the aqueducts would cost more than twice as much—between 120 billion and 130 billion lire (£80–86 million). Thus, argued Cortese, it would be necessary to establish a new set of priorities. The money raised by the Save Venice law would simply not be enough to achieve all that it proposed. Parts of the programme would have to be deferred until more cash became available. The only consolation was his evident faith that the money would eventually turn up. Indeed he added rather pointedly that the regional government had already budgeted the money which was due from Rome.

Adolfo Sarti, the man from Rome, spoke next, attempting to soothe anxieties with charm rather than facts, making the sort of speech which should be judged less by how it sounds than by the way it looks in the highlights recorded in a reporter's notebook. The residue of Sarti's speech was two warnings and a promise—'You must not bring such pressure as to create a lack of confidence . . . We cannot expect the immediate take-off of this new machinery . . . There will be a decisive step forward in September.'

No one could complain after the opening trio had sat down that the International Consultative Committee was being misled; the news was uniformly bad. There were grounds enough for Maheu to launch a swingeing attack on the Italian government, and go ahead and close the UNESCO office: everything that had been said sounded like a betrayal.

The diplomatic thing, however, was to put a brave face on it, and Maheu, looking pained, did just that. The language of diplomacy allowed Maheu to appear to delay comment on Sarti's speech; he would, he said, wait for a translation. He was comforting: of course there was a relationship between the nation's economic situation and the attempt to save Venice. Italy had only recently emerged from an appalling economic crisis during which it had to be saved from near bankruptcy by loans from America and Germany. It would be impossible to brush this aside, said Maheu: 'We should not start sending letters to Father Christmas.' But there was one thing he wanted to say: he had to point out that UNESCO's presence in Italy depended on the continued good will of its annual conference, and 'I cannot guarantee that it will accept forever a state of affairs in which we cannot produce results or even make encouraging noises.' Sarti nodded gravely, stayed for all the speeches—and obviously listened to them, since he switched on a smile whenever a delegate mentioned the embarrassment caused to all of them by the non-appearance of the government's loan money.

The members of the conference were, however, well bred (literally in the case of the English: there was not an untitled man among them), and there were no unseemly disputes for two days. By the third day, however, when it was still hot and Venice was beginning to smell a little, even the best-bred tempers began to fray, and there was a momentary hint that all was not well. It came when Sir Ashley Clarke raised the matter of tax.

Sir Ashley felt strongly that Venice in Peril and the other voluntary funds should be exempted from the value added tax, which the Italian government had insisted on imposing on all restoration bills at a rate of 12 per cent. This meant that

for each £10,000 collected for Venice in Britain, or anywhere else—not just from large donors but from the ten and
fifty pence pieces donated after a lecture in a village hall as
well—£1,200 went to the Italian exchequer.

Many Italians themselves deplored this apparent ingrati-
tude, even though VAT is a uniformily applied EEC, or
Common Market, tax, which means that American contributions to St Paul's or Canterbury Cathedral are similarly
taxed. The only hope of relief was if UNESCO would take
responsibility for the restoration work. The international
campaign for Venice is, after all, under UNESCO's umbrella.

Clarke got remarkably little sympathy from the Italians at
the conference. Bruno Visentini, who was shortly to become
Finance Minister, said that this was no time to be complaining about taxation. Maheu intervened: 'Do you mean that if
we help save the fabric of St Mark's, that money is taxed?'
Yes, was the reply from the government official, implying
that if the voluntary funds were to be in Venice, it was to be
on Rome's terms. At the time of writing, the issue is still
unsolved, though it looks as if tax exemptions through
UNESCO might eventually be granted.

Coming away from the meeting on the *traghetto* from San
Giorgio to the Riva degli Schiavoni, with the Ducal Palace
glowing in the evening sun, it was difficult to explain why
anyone had bothered to attend, except, of course, to admire
the view. If it was depressing inside the conference, it was no
less so outside, in Venice itself. Discussing the meeting with
local politicians in the finely restored surroundings of the
Querini-Stampalia, a library and gallery in which the Socialist
politician Giuseppe Mazzariol then had his office, the extent
of local hostility to UNESCO became disturbingly clear. It was

not anything UNESCO had done, but what it symbolized. 'The problem is 174 years old, but Maheu wants it solved by September,' said Mazzariol. 'We're not in such a hurry. We've made tremendous efforts to understand the problem, and we are getting fed up with all this Anglo-Saxon pragmatism. Give us time; the score is 0–0 at the moment.' It was a curious analogy, but if the struggle for Venice was a football match, it was difficult to leave the city that July without concluding that the forces ranged against the city, both natural and human, were not only winning, but that they were in a different and more powerful league.

It was as well that Maheu had not heard Mazzariol, for he was quintessentially French and to hear his intellectualism described as Anglo-Saxon pragmatism would, no doubt, have added insult to the injuries he had received during the conference. As it was, Maheu departed with the characteristic remark that: 'Personally I am very satisfied by the conclusions, but my satisfaction is still conditional.' He had been promised action by the end of September, before UNESCO's general conference met.

Unfortunately, on the day when the politicians involved in saving Venice were to meet in Rome that September, there was no longer a government in Rome to provide the politicians. By the time UNESCO's biennial general conference met in October, there were still no decisions. It was Maheu's last conference as Director-General, and just as there had been talk of his deciding to close the office in Venice before the July meeting, so there was further speculation that he would finally propose the closure this time. But Maheu's last act was to keep the operation alive. Anna Maria Cicogna had especially asked at the last meeting of the International Consultative Committee that Maheu be given honorary life membership, which was a pleasing gesture by a thoughtful lady, but Maheu could hardly have enjoyed the continuing spectacle over the next fifteen months that UNESCO's work provided.

The Commission to Safeguard Venice still met each month, and every month Joseph Martin was in loyal attendance, until he stopped living permanently in Venice in 1975. Many papers were noted, but few decisions were taken, and, ironically, UNESCO's presence was sometimes used by local politicians as a cover for their own failings. (For example, UNESCO was held partly responsible by men like Gianni de Michelis for the cancellation of a plan to convert the Saloni, a vast old salt warehouse on the Zattere, into a swimming pool when, in fact, the UNESCO office—sensing the political implications of the decision—had specifically decided not to intervene.)

The office was sometimes criticized abroad for failing to interest Venetians in the restoration of the city. But that was not how the office had been conceived. When it was first thought of by Maheu he had assumed, optimistically, that by the mid-1970s there would be an ambitious international operation to save Venice, and that the office would provide high powered management and co-ordination. It was hardly UNESCO's fault that these ambitions remained unfulfilled, but it did force the organization to change the emphasis of its Venice operation: cultural events like the ballet festival in 1975 were organized, and expert reports on Venetian town planning commissioned.

So what had UNESCO achieved in Venice during Maheu's eight years in office? The Save Venice law had been passed, but most of it had not been implemented. The fight over value added tax went on. And the idea that Venice was in crisis had spread into the most unexpected corners of the world, as the list of countries which had issued special postage stamps in support of the Save Venice campaign showed (it included such unlikely supporters as Burundi, the Ivory Coast, Gabon, Upper Volta, Mali, Mauritania, Niger, New Caledonia, the Khmer Republic, Togo, Dahomey, Cameroon and Chad). It was difficult not to conclude that Maheu had retired a disappointed man, and when he died in December 1975, only fifteen months after leaving UNESCO, the event was scarcely noticed in Italy. There was a paragraph in *Corriere della Sera*, a few brief words elsewhere, and no representative of the Italian government attended his funeral.

Shortly before he retired, Maheu sat on the terrace of the Bauer Grunwald Hotel on the Grand Canal and explained to us the strict limitations of UNESCO's role in Venice. Why had he been so diplomatic in the face of bureaucratic obscurantism? 'Because if there is no confidence, there is no partnership. An international civil servant like me must trust the member state.'

What had he concluded about Venice's future? 'My greatest worry is that I do not see enough signs of cultural activities.' The Fenice opera house was shut then; the Biennale was uncertain of itself and its future; the craftsmen that UNESCO had hoped would settle in Venice had not done so. Even the gondola industry was fighting for survival. Maheu wondered about the *Gazzettino*, Venice's daily paper, whose copies had to be distributed by large barges instead of lorries: would it move out? (It later turned out that it would— another migrant to Mestre.) Next he worried about the shortage of men capable of doing the work necessary to save the fabric of the city. 'We can find out what is going to fall down, but we haven't got the people to prevent it from doing so.' Why not? 'Man,' Maheu replied sadly, 'is the greatest obstacle to human progress, because of his obstinacy.'

But if the attempt to save Venice had not worked so far, might it not be the time for UNESCO to take the initiative, organize a great international fund, and gather a collection of international experts to take over the job? Maheu shook his head. 'No', he said, 'UNESCO could not do that; it is not equipped to raise the money, nor to disburse it efficiently. It would also create an impossible imbalance in UNESCO's activities. It was not conceived for this kind of thing. The world is not organized in such a way, and it would be unwise of UNESCO to think it is. We have no right to intervene without partnership.' Maheu paused before he concluded: 'The Italians must save Venice.' And would they? 'They must. They have a duty to save Venice for the world.'

CHAPTER 9

The International Crusade

IT was all very well for René Maheu to argue that the Italians must save Venice, but in the years after 1966 they were transparently failing to do so, and much of the work that was being visibly undertaken in the city was financed and organized by foreign groups. They have become a primary repository of experience, and talking to them is as good a way as any of finding out what needs to be done, what difficulties there are, and whether it is feasible to save Venice by voluntary effort. We take four cases here, each illustrating a different facet of the city's agony.

The winter of 1974–5 was a period of unemployment and inflation in Europe, bleak for almost everyone, but especially so for those whose job was to raise money. Throughout 1974 funds for organizations like Britain's Venice in Peril had almost completely dried up. There had been two ways of raising the money for the major items of its work—the restoration of the churches of San Nicolo and the Madonna dell'Orto, and Sansovino's Loggetta at the base of the campanile in St Mark's Square. The first method involved VIP's chairman, Lord Norwich, lecturing to groups in school and church halls, and hoping that the message would inspire his audience to contribute. It was not an easy task. Norwich had to persuade the donors that Venice is in poor enough shape to justify their contributing some money to saving it, but not in such poor shape, or so corrupt, as to make a contribution a waste of money. (He had a bad time in the months after the revelations about the Venice loan.)

The second way of raising money was easier, but less reliable. It was the hope of a large donation, or a sudden flood of postal contributions after the plight of Venice had been exposed once more in a newspaper or, much better, on television. But in 1974 neither way was producing enough money. Norwich even started to contribute his own lecture fees, and desperate appeals had to be made to restore the organ at San Nicolo, the final job needing to be done there. By the end of the year the state of Venice in Peril's finances was so parlous that the committee was discussing closing the office in the old army barracks in Kensington, even though it cost a mere £6 a week. Some of the committee argued that it was, perhaps, no bad thing. They had done distinguished work, and, after all, the Italian government had passed laws investing itself with responsibility for saving Venice. Even Sir Ashley Clarke, who had performed so manfully in Venice itself, had resigned himself to the termination of his work there.

Then, in the first months of 1975, everything changed. The trustees of the Sainsbury Foundation, which is connected to the successful grocery chain, decided to give £50,000 ($100,000) to Venice in Peril—the biggest single donation it had ever received. Shortly afterwards London Weekend Television devoted two successive programmes to Venice, cleverly linking a gondola race down the Grand Canal with the race to save its buildings and paintings. At the end of each programme the address of Venice in Peril was shown on the screen, and appeals made for money. It was an advertisement which would have cost a corporation thousands of pounds, and it raised some £20,000 for Venice in Peril.

The pressing problem became what to spend the Sainsbury money on. Discussions consumed the spring and summer of 1975, with each of the most active members lobbying, in the most discreet and gentlemanly way, for his favourite proposal. Then in July, the Sainsbury Foundation sent its own man, Tim Sainsbury, to see Venice for himself and decide where the money should go.

One factor which eventually dictates choice is the vision of the people who make it, and the most ambitious idea was conceived by John Hale, Professor of Italian at University College, London, a historian by trade, and a student of Venetian military history during the Renaissance who had learned his way around the extensive Venetian archives which stretch out behind the Frari. (He was also chairman of the trustees of the National Gallery in London, and therefore not ignorant of Venetian painting either.) A military historian in Venice is most concerned with naval history, and central to the sea defences of Venice since the sixteenth century has been the Forte di Sant'Andrea at the eastern side of the Lido entrance to the lagoon. It is an imposing place, much admired by Giulio Lorenzetti, who states in his guide:

This is an important work, not only for its military merits, but also for the architectural beauty of its severe monumental rusticated façade which has been left much as it was except for some additions made in 1570–71, the years of the victory of Lepanto. This is commemorated in an inscription mounted on a Lion passant. Unfortunately one side of the fort has crumbled, and it is to be hoped it will be rebuilt, and restored.

This could have been the text for Hale's case for Venice in Peril spending its £50,000 on the Forte di Sant'Andrea. By 1975, the state of the fort was much worse than Lorenzetti had observed. The tides rush in and batter the base on which the fort was built; the physical position of the building intensifies the damage by turning the tide into a whirlpool, which scours away more of its foundations. If nothing were done to the foundations, a major part of the fort would collapse into the sea. And if nothing were done to preserve the structure itself, it too would deteriorate. If it were in Venice itself, the case of the fort would have been taken up years ago. But no public transport goes there, and unless you hire a launch it can only be seen across the channel from the Lido.

Hale is an ingenious debater, and his plan made a virtue of all these limitations. He proposed that Venice in Peril should prepare plans not just for the preservation of the fort, but for the development of the island by opening restaurants and designing walks, perhaps even building a small yacht basin. The preparatory work would be intended to stimulate the Italian government into taking up the project, and the city council into providing a *vaporetto* service during the summer. It was all rather grand—too grand, some of Hale's colleagues thought. Venice in Peril would be able to afford only a small percentage of the cost, so the credit for doing it would inevitably go elsewhere and, since it is important to have something to show to contributors who like to be able to see how their money has been spent, the difficulty of access would also count against it.

Sir Ashley Clarke was a good deal less ambitious. He lived in Venice, and knew the concerns of the Superintendents, especially Francesco Valcanover, who had an apartment in the same building as him, and as the man in charge of the preservation of paintings, was becoming concerned about the condition of four very special works by Tintoretto. They are on the walls of the anti-Collegio of the Ducal Palace, where the ambassadors to Venice, and the city's own diplomats, would wait to be heard by the councillors who ran the Serene Republic. Lorenzetti describes the four large paintings done in 1578 as 'Tintoretto reaching the highest expression of his art in these masterpieces.'

The trouble is that the lustrous colour is deteriorating, and will continue to do so unless the paintings are restored. What particularly appealed to Sir Ashley was that restoration would enable Venice in Peril to use again the laboratory of San Gregorio, which it had earlier helped to establish. This was a disused church big enough to house the vast Tintorettos which had to be cleaned after the 1966 floods. A chemical laboratory was installed too, but it had run out of steam by the mid-1970s. The laboratory was not well lit, and very cold in winter; nevertheless, Sir Ashley believed that the decision to restore the Tintorettos from the anti-Collegio would breathe life into San Gregorio again.

There were other arguments in favour of his plan. Valcanover thought restoration might reveal some more painting by Tintoretto, and if Venice in Peril did the anti-Collegio it was possible that Valcanover might be able to persuade the government in Rome to pay for the restoration of the paintings in the Collegio itself, next door.

The problems of the Ducal Palace, the building that was

the wonder of mediaeval Europe, are not confined to the interior paintings. Over the main entrance there is a scaffolding on the stonework above the gate to prevent loose chips of stone falling on the heads of unsuspecting visitors. The gateway is known as the Porta della Carta, and the decorative work is so detailed that Lorenzetti described it as being more like that of a goldsmith than an architect. It was started in 1438, and in the fifteenth and sixteenth centuries was gorgeously decorated in blue and gold. The paint faded long ago, and now the stone itself is crumbling away. It was another contender for the Venice in Peril £50,000, especially as it stands opposite the Loggetta, which had been completed in 1974, and would therefore give a geographical unity to vip's work.

Its supporters were mainly London-based. Lord Norwich and Sir John Pope-Hennessy were keen, so was Lady Thorneycroft, wife of a Conservative politician, an Italian who had herself been brought up in Venice. The reason was that the Porta della Carta would utilize the talents of Kenneth Hempel, a stone restorer at the Victoria and Albert Museum, who had been involved in restoration work of this kind ever since Sir John had sent him to Florence in 1966. Lately, he had concentrated on Venice and had trained a young Italian, Giulia Musumeci, whose salary had been paid by Venice in Peril. They had worked together on the Loggetta, and made a formidable team.

The same case could be made for the central Gothic arch of St Mark's Cathedral, which disappeared behind a scaffold in the summer of 1973 because it, too, was crumbling away. Hempel and Musumeci were keen to do the job of restoration and conservation. For both, the stonework on the façade of the Cathedral offered the greatest challenge to their

Heroes of Venice's last days: Kenneth Hempel of the Victoria and Albert Museum, who is battling to save the stone, and Roberto Frassetto, a dedicated scientist whose plans to save the lagoon have come to nothing.

Giulia Musumeci painstakingly cleaning the Loggetta at the Campanile in St Mark's Square. *Below* the Loggetta as it was before she started work on it, and *bottom* transformed.

Venice in Peril's triumph – the interior of the church of San Nicolo dei Mendicoli during restoration. *Below* Sir Ashley Clarke, VIP's Venice representative who supervised the work, with the restored church in the background.

How much longer can Venice be propped up? If nothing is done our children will be the last to see the Venice we know.

own skills, but the *proto* of St Mark's—the man in charge of
the maintenance of the structure—was slow to make up his
mind. Then he died, and nothing was decided during the
interregnum. Given time to think about it, the enthusiasm of
committee-men like Lord Norwich for this project faded
because, after all, the Cathedral itself was wealthy and could
afford its own restoration work.

There was one other contender at the beginning: the great
mosaic of the Teotoca Madonna, the mother of God, in the
cathedral on the island of Torcello in the north of the lagoon
—the first real link between Byzantium and western Europe.
The mosaic is stunningly simple, undoubtedly one of the
most beautiful things in Venice. After six hundred years, the
cement between the mosaic pieces has begun to decay, and
the whole mosaic needs restoration.

Sainsbury's July tour had very distinguished guides: Lord
Norwich and Sir John Pope-Hennessy had flown out from
London with him, and in Venice they were joined by Renato
Padoan, the Superintendent of Monuments. One project had
not survived the journey. John Hale's enthusiasm for the
Forte di Sant'Andrea was not shared. It was too big and too
far away from the centre of activity, the team concluded.
Sainsbury had a bias in favour of the Torcello mosaics before
going to Venice, but the visit undermined it. Sir John thought
Torcello an élitist place, mostly seen by a few visitors after a
good lunch at the Locanda Cipriani. Moreover, he argued
that it would be fruitless to restore the mosaics while the
building itself remained damp, and to dry out that great
cathedral would surely cost more money than they had.
There was doubt too, about how the mosaics would be
restored: whether it would be necessary to remove them—
an extremely delicate operation—or whether they could be

done where they were. It was clearly going to be a big job: too big, they decided.

The choice now narrowed to the projects in and around St Mark's Square. The paintings inside the Ducal Palace were considered, but Sainsbury's interests involved architecture more than painting. So when the case for the Porta della Carta was considered, Sainsbury listened attentively. Hempel had reported that the entrance to the Ducal Palace was in even worse shape than they previously thought; Sainsbury thought it a very lovely piece of high Venetian Gothic, and knew the Foundation would be pleased by the fact that the costs could be properly controlled, and the work undertaken quickly.

At lunch on the second day of their visit they all went to the Locanda Montin, a restaurant much used by English visitors. Sainsbury announced that the money would go to the Porta della Carta, and he hoped work would begin in the autumn. It seemed a satisfactory conclusion. The sad thing for Venice was that only one project could be chosen. The rest would have to find other sponsors or else continue to rot.

Much of the activity of foreign organizations involves quite complex construction work, securing buildings from flooding, or simply preventing them from falling down. A job of this magnitude had been taken on by one of the two American organizations involved in Venice, Save Venice Inc., run by a Bostonian called John MacAndrew who taught at the girls' college at Wellesley. He is a historian and a collector of beautiful churches, and the biggest item in his collection is the Gesuiti. Built between 1715 and 1728, it had reached such a stage of disrepair that it was in danger of falling into the canal that runs along its east wall. The 1973 UNESCO survey stated that 'at the time of writing this church is perhaps in the greatest danger of any in Venice.'

The church is an astonishing spectacle, decorated in green and white marquetry which looks like expensive wallpaper until you get close to it and discover it is all marble. The huge baroque altar with a *baldacchino*, or small dome, is supported by ten twisted columns, and the tabernacle is made of lapis lazuli. The altar is surrounded by four huge piers or pillars. The weight of the whole thing is immense—so great that the wall behind the altar had begun to slip away at the base. At the back of the church long bores had been taken from foundations and they revealed a structure 15 feet deep, starting with carefully laid bricks and mortar; beneath this was a layer of stone, and then some rough rubble. Under that there was a platform of oak timbers in two layers, still in good condition, and then the oak piles, driven 7 feet into the clay.

The solution seemed straightforward enough to Mac-Andrew and Renato Padoan: the earth beneath the east wall was moving into the canal because of the weight of the building. If new piles were driven deeper into the clay the movement would stop, and the Gesuiti would be saved. The plans were drawn up: thirty-eight piles would be driven in on the outer side of the wall, inclined slightly from the vertical so that a pile which began on the outside of the wall would come out underneath the foundation below the inside of the wall. Another thirty-four piles would be driven from the inside of the wall, finishing up on the outside. The result would be a criss-cross of concrete piles, each forty-two feet long, mainly under the heavy altar.

At this stage, early in 1974, there arrived in Venice from the US an old man called Robert Maccoun. He too was a

New Englander, and had grown up in shipyards along the Atlantic coast where he had worked as an engineer; after the war he had settled in Paris and became a successful consultant. Maccoun came to Venice with nothing specific in mind, beyond a general feeling that he had some skills and enough to live on, and that if he could do anything to help Venice, so much the better: 'It is too important just to let it go.' Maccoun met MacAndrew, asked if he could help, and was told that he most certainly could. MacAndrew would be particularly grateful if Maccoun would look through the records of the Gesuiti at the Superintendent's office, and see if anything interesting emerged. Maccoun said he would, but he talked to the contractor first. 'I saw then that I could do much more good simply by observing problems on the site.' During January and February 1975, he went there every working day, and at the end of it produced a report which suggested that the problem was not as simple as it had appeared to MacAndrew, Padoan and the contractor.

The first thing was to diagnose the problem correctly, he said. The real trouble was the cracks in the abutment walls which connected the wall by the canal to the nearest of the piers surrounding the altar. Priests at the church said they had been there for some time, but had grown markedly worse since the 1966 floods. Next Maccoun wanted to find out exactly why the movement which had caused the cracks had taken place. Before his arrival there had been no doubt about the reason: the massive baroque altar was so heavy that the foundations were insufficient to hold it, and its weight was forcing the clay underneath the foundations to move sideways into the canal, taking the wall with it. But Maccoun looked around him, and wondered about the four green and white marquetry pillars which surrounded the altar. Looking up he saw that they had to support the roof and the clerestory wall. Surely they must be creating pressure on the foundations too. But they had not been included in previous calculations. Maccoun started doing some of his own, and worked out that while the altar weight was about 320 tons, the weight of each of these piers was 470 tons. So the piers were putting six times more pressure on the foundations than the altar. Moreover, the original foundations under the piers were not as substantial as the foundations under the altar.

The implications of that conclusion were frightening: Maccoun feared that the restoration as planned could actually hasten the destruction of the church. If the main pressure on the clay underneath the foundations came from the piers and not the altar, the new piles driven in to stop movement created only by the weight of the altar would not be enough, and the clay under the piers would go on moving, but probably at two different rates, thus putting the foundations of the church under intolerable stress.

'The reason for the mix-up,' Maccoun concluded, 'is a basic disinclination to go and look for expert engineering advice. Padoan, for instance, is content to let the contractor decide what to do. Contractors are anxious to do well, but their first reaction is to do what will get by. When they're pushed they don't mind. But what is really wrong is that there is no one capable of ordering a specification, then supervising the job.'

Maccoun concluded his report with three proposals for preventing further movement caused by pressure from the four great piers, but each would involve considerably more work, and more expense; and therein lay the rub. Organizations like Save Venice Inc. tend to undertake projects such as the Gesuiti with not quite enough money for the repairs that the Superintendent believes are necessary. The preoccupation of devoted men like MacAndrew is, quite naturally, to raise the money, not to deal with the engineering problems. When given the report, MacAndrew did as much as Save Venice could do to meet its proposals, but there was not enough cash to meet them all and most of the work had to be done to MacAndrew's original specifications. 'Any trouble will come after the contractor and John MacAndrew are dead,' says Maccoun philosophically. But the original concept of the operation—to stop the Gesuiti falling into the canal—had rather longer term objectives than that.

No private individual has worked harder at raising funds for Venice than Colonel James A. Gray (US Army retd.), and no one has succeeded so well. James A. Gray is the executive director of the International Fund for Monuments, which is the most high-powered of the voluntary societies. The IFM was established by Gray in 1965 because the Easter Island stone heads were in danger, and Gray went about the task of saving them with military precision. (He had a distinguished war in intelligence, being among the first Americans in Sicily after the invasion; later he became one of the military attachés at the American Embassy in Rome, married an Italian, and was wounded in Korea before finally leaving the army.) The IFM's offices are in New York City, in Gramercy Park, and from there Gray fires off a series of newsletters to his contributors. The letters are a fine illustration of the scope and drive of the Colonel's work for Venice.

The first, dated 31 May 1969, was still more concerned with Easter Island and its stone statues than with the stones of Venice, but the last page mentions the Venice Committee of the IFM, which had been formed in February largely because of the 'interest and fund raising efforts of Professor John MacAndrew'. Gray made a number of points about the Venice operation: 'The Committee has a logically thought out and workable program for the rescue of this art'; moreover, 'Contributions go *net* to the actual work in Venice since IFM is taking care of the administrative overhead'; and, finally, 'Disbursements are rigorously controlled.' It was clear, then, from the very beginning, that Colonel Gray wanted IFM to be the biggest and the best, and that when its work began in the summer of 1969 with the restoration of the great series of paintings by Tintoretto in the Scuola di San Rocco, nothing was going to be left to chance.

The next newsletter, sent on 30 April 1970, began this time with Venice, and Gray announced that the city was rapidly becoming the primary concern of the IFM. The form of organization of IFM had been determined—a series of independent cells, not unlike an underground political party, but described instead as chapters. There was one in Los Angeles, another in Boston, one in Washington DC, and others were being discussed for Cleveland, Detroit, St Louis, San Francisco, and Durham, North Carolina. Again, Gray insisted that since the IFM was picking up the bill for administration, all the money went to Venice. It was, he said, 'a truly unique and efficient arrangement'. The sums involved were substantial. The first estimate for cleaning the Tintorettos was $200,000. Gray got most of it from the Edgar J. Kaufmann Trust, Pittsburg. There was a hint of criticism of the Italian government, to which Gray had been willing to leave the solution of the major engineering problems. He mentioned in passing the 'rather protracted study of the problems confronting Venice.'

By the following year IFM had really got going. Gray

wrote his report en route to New York after a week in Venice, and the news was good. There had been a high tide which had covered St Mark's Square with a foot of water the week before, 'but lest the reader interpret this as indications of the early demise of Venice, it is sufficient to call attention to the soaring prices of real estate and the high rents for even modest apartments—a true indicator of the future well-being of the city.' This optimistic note was not surprising. IFM had introduced a courtesy discount card as a way of raising funds. The card cost $20 but entitled the holder to discounts at hotels, restaurants and shops. As Gray pointed out, 'At today's prices, it doesn't take many visits to a restaurant to get back (at 10 per cent) the minimum contribution.' Gray described a school teacher in a small midwestern town who had written to him that she had been to Venice many years ago, and might never achieve her dream to return, but that she treasured the card which she would keep to show her children and grandchildren that she did not sit idly by while that lovely city was lost to them.

By now the list of projects was growing fast. Gray announced that he had taken on the job of restoring the Scuola di San Giovanni Evangelista, a substantial palace built in the fourteenth and fifteenth centuries, containing a fine stairway and a great hall, with a good eighteenth-century marble floor, and a slightly overbearing altar. The building was in poor shape, and had been closed after the 1966 floods because of the danger of its falling into the canal, which ran along one of its walls. The restoration programme began in 1970 with repairs to the roof. After that the IFM began looking for the money to make the building flood-proof from the canals by encasing the interior of the building with two thicknesses of lead. But there was a bonus in the decision to repair the Scuola. Behind the altar in the great hall were two offices, and Gray commandeered them for the IFM. A plasterer was brought in to restore them in the Venetian style of pastel pink, green and yellow, and soon the Fund was the only organization to have an office in Venice with a telephone, a boiler to heat the place, and eventually— distinguishing them from the other voluntary groups— a photo-copying machine.

That was not all. Work was also beginning in the Pieta ('on the Riva degli Schiavoni, east of the Hotel Danieli'), and at Santa Maria del Giglio ('the well known church near the Gritti Palace'); the Los Angeles chapter had adopted the church of San Pietro di Castello, and Boston the Scuola dei Carmini. The Fund was also on the look-out for a chapter which would help with the Schola Canton in the Ghetto. The fund-raising cards were going well, Gray having been told that the theme of Noah and the dove was 'very appropriate to the times'. There was only one slightly sour note in the whole newsletter. It was the suggestion that a schism had taken place in the American effort to save Venice. Professor John MacAndrew, it was announced, had 're-signed because of policy differences'. In fact, MacAndrew not only resigned, he set up the rival Save Venice Inc. John MacAndrew was never mentioned again in the newsletter; nor was the new rival organization.

The next newsletter came two years later on 18 May 1973, a gap Gray explained by a near disaster with mailing. 'At the last minute it was not possible to get the letters aboard the *Christophoro Colombo* as planned, so they were put into the Italian postal system which thereupon went on strike.' As a result, the Fund was left with an awful lot of unsold Christmas cards on its hands. Otherwise the news was good; the

Special Law to Save Venice had been passed a month earlier, and Gray was on the verge of a major discovery: the problems of Venice were not the floods, or the air pollution (he had previously announced that Venice had the cleanest air of any Western city). It was the pigeons.

> I am much more concerned about damage by pigeons than I am about high water. So far, all efforts to bring the pigeon population under control have hardly kept up to the birthrate but have stirred up a great deal of controversy—so much so that the Italian government publicly denied that the pigeons in Venice were being sold to restaurants. In my opinion the problem will eventually be solved by treating the stone surfaces so as to render them impervious to the corrosive action of pigeon droppings.

Pigeons were still his preoccupation in the next newsletter, sent on 1 January 1974.

> In my opinion, the greatest damage to the stone of Venice is caused by the pigeons which the Austrians unwittingly introduced during the occupation about a hundred and fifty years ago. Over the past three years there have been a number of meetings to discuss the pigeon problem. Amongst measures considered to control their population was the use of chemically treated corn which renders the eggs infertile, but a study of the costs indicated that this method is too expensive. My proposal to exchange 1000 Venetian pigeons for 100 of Emperor Haile Selassie's Ethiopian pigeon hawks was not taken seriously. The daily feeding in Piazza San Marco was discontinued on 1 January 1973, and the pigeons have had a difficult year with 15 per cent fewer tourists . . . The birds are looking

more scraggly than ever but it is comforting to know that for many of them the suffering may soon be over. In a meeting in the Mayor's office on 11 December a specialized firm in Torino was authorized to undertake a full scale netting programme which proponents predict will reduce the pigeon population from 400,000 to less than 5,000 . . . It is a humane and effective programme carried out with the full approval of the local equivalent of the SPCA, but it could easily be sabotaged by over-eager journalists.

But the next newsletter had bad news:

The pigeon netting which was initiated last December was suspended in April, presumably because of pressure from nature lovers. In announcing that the programme had materially thinned out the pigeon population with the capture of 25,000, the city's hygiene department added that it had imported a number of French pigeons to strengthen the breed since the Venetian pigeons are so scraggy. This announcement is discouraging to those of us who witness the great damage done by the birds to monuments in this city.

Gray was back to the subject again in his newsletter on 10 January 1975. This time the news was worse: the IFM had earlier been most enthusiastic about the possibility of a contraceptive pill for pigeons (the drug firm GD Searle had produced one called Ornitrol). Gray wrote:

A September 11 report from Versailles reveals that, despite massive feeding of oral contraceptives over the past two years, the pigeon population has increased. Authorities there have suspended use of the pill pending examination of 200 pigeons to determine what went

123

wrong. Another failure of pigeon control is reported from Ravenna where several pairs of falcons were released and carefully observed. The authorities were disappointed to discover that the falcons each killed only one pigeon daily and that the falcon droppings are much larger and far more corrosive than those of pigeons.

Gray's quixotic attitude to the unenthusiastic, the critics, and the reporters—'the enemies of Venice'—let alone the pigeons, tended to obscure the remarkable achievements of the Fund. In 1975 the office, which had now been elevated into an information centre for visitors to Venice, was able to put out a map of the city which showed fourteen separate projects undertaken by the IFM. The first great job—the Tintorettos at the Scuola di San Rocco—had finally been completed; so had the major restoration of San Pietro di Castello, largely paid for by an elderly lady in Los Angeles. Many of the chapters that had been established in the early 1970s had completed small restorations, often of paintings, and the major work at the Scuola di San Giovanni Evangelista was coming along well, with the first vital stage involving the water-proofing and protection of the building entirely completed. It was an impressive achievement; it could compensate for the fact that Colonel James A. Gray had not made a great many friends in Venice, especially among the people involved in the same business as himself. But of him, perhaps more than of any of them, it could be said as it was said of Christopher Wren in St Paul's: 'Si monumentum requiris, circumspice.' (If you require a monument to him, look around.)

The best known Venetian of all is the Merchant, Shylock,

and he never existed in the flesh. Shylock is not even a character in the long folk memory of the Jewish ghetto in Venice. Mention Shylock to a Venetian Jew and he will dismiss Shakespeare with some scorn: Jessica could not possibly have eloped with Lorenzo, he will tell you firmly, because the gates of the ghetto were locked every night, and guarded by four Christians.

The Venice ghetto still exists, though most of the Jews left in the nineteenth century after King Victor Emanuel II relaxed all residential restrictions on them. The *campo* of the Ghetto Nuovo is one of the bleakest in the city, large, windswept and surrounded by taller buildings than elsewhere. These are often in a poor state of repair, but even on the finest days the ghetto induces a feeling of anxiety in a visitor, perhaps because the Venetian ghetto is a permanent reminder of the intolerance of Christian Europeans towards the Jews. It seems fitting, therefore, that a mysterious German has offered to pay a major part of the cost of restoring the oldest synagogue in the ghetto, the Schola Grande Tedesca.

The Schola Grande Tedesca was begun in 1528, twelve years after the Venetian government had ruled that Jews could live permanently in Venice, instead of applying for constant renewal of their permits to do so. But the condition was that they should all live in one place. It was the first ruling of its kind in Europe, and the place has since given its name to all similar areas; it was in the San Cirolamo district, and the island on which the Jews were to live was the site of an abandoned foundry for iron casting. The Venetian for cast is *getar*, corrupted to geto, further corrupted to ghetto. They are matter-of-fact about it today in the office of the Israeli community in the old ghetto, the Ghetto Vecchio, and one of its leaders, an accountant called Giorgio Voghera, says: 'If you have to worship three times a day you are obviously going to live near the places of worship.' In fact, life in the ghetto was infinitely preferable to the enforced nomadic existence of the Jews in earlier centuries. But in 1288 the Jews were banished to Mestre, and for the next couple of centuries could visit Venice only if they had a permit. They were also forced to wear an identifying mark —first a yellow O on their chests, and later a cap, first yellow, then red. The creation of the ghetto allowed them to establish a community, and build the synagogues, or *schole*; five of them survive, all but one of them in extremely poor condition.

The Schola Grande Tedesca is in a corner of the Ghetto Nuovo; it is approached through a museum in which the relics of 400 years of Jewish life in Venice are preserved, up a staircase to the top of the house. The synagogues are usually at the top of the house, not because of some obscure religious ritual, as some scholars suggest, but because it was nice to get above ground level and admit a bit of light into the place. But it does mean that the process of restoration is uncommonly slow, since it has to begin some floors down from the Schola, in the basement, in order to prevent the building from falling into the canal.

The Schola Grande Tedesca is oval shaped, surrounded by elegant wooden seating, and marmorino decorations on the walls; the pulpit at one end of the room is much gilded, and there is an atmosphere of ornate decoration—the Jews were Venetians, and they saw no reason why they should not worship in some style. A gallery hangs from the wall, built to accommodate the women, and the gravest structural problem is the roof above this gallery. In the eighteenth century the synagogue was restored, and new roof beams put in; two centuries later they were placing considerable pressure on the walls on the *campo* and canal sides of the building, forcing them outwards. If they were allowed to go on doing so the walls would collapse. Replacing these beams is made considerably more difficult by the fact that the eighteenth-century restorers omitted to take the original beams out. In addition, the women's gallery is attached to the new beams and is sinking, which makes it possible that the roof will fall in before it pushes the walls out. To prevent all this is challenging work; damp and eroded foundations are common enough in Venice, but work on the roof is more difficult. Nevertheless, there are detailed plans to place reinforced concrete in the 20-inch walls and fix new beams into the concrete.

A further problem is the floor. Like St Mark's, it is both made of marble, and irregular—there is a difference of some 10 inches in the floor level in different parts of the synagogue. It is a characteristic of Venetian building that the walls tend to sink. The reason for the waves in the synagogue floor is that some foundation walls beneath it, which help to support it, have sunk and others have not. The most obvious trouble on the floor is the effect of salinity and humidity on the marble, which is beginning to crumble badly. 'It's like old age,' says Voghera philosophically, 'the older the building, the less capable it is of bearing the strains on it.'

The cost of restoration is considerable: the architect estimates that it will come to 100 million lire (£66,000), not the kind of money that the Israeli community can raise itself, and American Jewry has turned out, somewhat unexpectedly, to be a poor source of funds. So it was as welcome as it was unexpected when, in 1974, Giorgio Voghera heard that a

German businessman was willing to provide 75 million lire (£50,000). This would mean that the major structural work could be undertaken. The offer had come through German businessmen in Milan, and one of the conditions was that it should be an anonymous act of reparation.

It would be quite wrong, of course, to assume that only American and British funds go to save Venice. Apart from the anonymous German businessman, there is a German National Commission, headed by an ex-Ambassador to Italy, Hans von Herwarth. The Germans have been unlucky; the centrepiece of their operation was the Miracoli, which has turned out to be a disastrous piece of restoration, though their reputation for efficiency was partly retrieved by a splendid restoration at the Palazzo Barberigo della Terrazza.

The French come and go, in a style described unsympathetically by one of the Anglo-Saxons as 'flying in, plonking a big cheque on the altar, and praising God for France.' The largest cheque was placed on the not inconsiderable altar of Santa Maria della Salute, the most painted church in Venice after St Mark's itself and standing just behind the Customs House, whose famous gilded ball is also a product of recent restoration. The Salute provided the most graphic illustration of the state of stone in Venice; at an early stage of the restoration, when there was still a serious danger that the statues might crumble and plunge to the ground, a notice was put up outside the church warning: 'Beware, falling angels.' The French Committee, headed by Gaston Palewski, an old Gaullist, planned one other job which is to its eternal credit. All other committees have concentrated on churches and *scuole*; the French looked at the possibility of restoring a famous eighteenth-century whorehouse, the Ridotto della Procuratoressa Venier—a perfectly proper thing to do historically, since during its greatest days Venice was as famous throughout Europe for its prostitution as it was for its art and architecture.

There are other Save Venice committees in Holland, Belgium, Luxemburg, Switzerland, Australia and Iran. (It would be historically appropriate if the Arabs were to use their oil wealth to help save Venice since it was the Venetians who, by opening European markets for the spices from Arabia eight centuries ago, created the last Arab economic boom.)

Lastly, there are the Italians themselves. Apart from the government, nine separate organizations have contributed something towards restoration. Some, like the Banco San Marco, which gilded the ball on the Customs House, took on only one project; others, like the insurance company, Assicurazioni di Trieste e Venezia, had good ideas which never came to pass. They had intended cleaning the Procuratie Vecchie, one whole side of St Mark's Square (the Quadri's side), but Superintendent Padoan decided that cleaning would spoil the patina on the stone, a curious decision since he had allowed other buildings to be cleaned. But there is no appeal against the Superintendent.

The Comitato per il Centro Storico Ebraico di Venezia never got its proposed restoration of the Schola Italiana going, and its cracked windows add to the air of general dilapidation in the *campo* in the Ghetto Nuova. The Societa Dante Alighieri cleaned the great gate to the Arsenale, but, according to the experts, did so rather clumsily.

There is something about restoring Venice which seems to induce unusually strong internal tensions in the groups which

E   129

organize it, and the Italians have suffered from schisms—and internecine strife—much as the Americans did. The whole campaign to save Venice started in 1959, long before the disastrous flood, with Italia Nostra. This began to compile the list of endangered Venetian *palazzi* which UNESCO later completed. Venezia Nostra was the major group to splinter from Italia Nostra, and its one project is among the easiest to see, since anyone taking a *vaporetto* on the Grand Canal passes underneath it. Venezia Nostra are restoring the Rialto bridge.

The most productive of the Italian funds, however, is the Comitato Italiano per Venezia, run by Bruno Visentini, which has to its credit the most striking act of restoration in Venice. In September 1971 five paintings by Giovanni Bellini and Bartolomeo Vivarini were stolen from San Giovanni e Paolo. The Comitato immediately offered a reward of five million lire (£3,300). The paintings were returned as quickly and mysteriously as they had been taken. Restoring Venice has never been so quick or so simple.

CHAPTER IO

One Man's Work

IT is a tribute to the commitment of the volunteers from abroad that they do not seem to question whether in the long run their work is worthwhile. To outsiders who brood on the Special Law, the loan, the self-interest and the cynicism with which the story is littered, this might seem naive. But to the workers who have tackled a particular problem, beaten it, and restored a piece of Venice there is no doubt. There is a perfect case of this, down by the docks, in a poor area, full of small stores and bars, and squat fourteenth-century slum houses. Washing hangs out of the windows, canaries sing endlessly and, eventually, the narrow alleys give way to a small courtyard containing a flagpole, a wellhead, a stone column, a few scrawny trees, and an old church.

The church is San Nicolo dei Mendicoli, and it has been restored by Britain's Venice in Peril. But the work is not the corporate act of an international organization. It has been the personal preoccupation of Venice in Peril's resident vice-chairman, Sir Ashley Clarke, and to hear from him the story of the restoration of San Nicolo is to grasp quite clearly the way the voluntary bodies believe they can best help Venice.

When Clarke first saw San Nicolo early in 1967, it was the despair of its priest and its congregation. It is surrounded on three sides by two small canals, the Rio San Nicolo and the

Rio delle Terese. When the water in these canals rose the church would flood, not gently and gradually, but with a violence that sent water spouting through cracks in the marble floor. When the flood water subsided, there was no relief, because rain would come through holes in the roof. Pigeons came through the same holes and the weight of their excrement made the paintings on the ceiling sag. In the winter the church was rarely dry and never warm. The congregation was declining, the paintings on the walls were deteriorating and the wooden statues that could just be glimpsed in the gloom were dirty, neglected, and being eaten by worms. If nothing was done, the people who breathed life into the church would gradually abandon it. In a way it was just like Venice.

San Nicolo's history is a recital of disaster and recovery, victory and defeat. It was founded in the seventh century, possibly on the site of a fort, and named after Saint Nicholas, an eastern hero who is not only the original Santa Claus, but also patron saint of scholars, the poor and, most important of all, fishermen—because San Nicolo was founded by fishermen, descendants of those early Venetians who had fled to the islands in the lagoon. As time went on it became the centre of a tight little community which had its own Doge and standard. Its members called themselves the Nicolotti, after their church. The priest there now, a small, rotund and exuberant man called Father Scarpa, has written a history of San Nicolo, from its records, which go back to 1337. From this one learns that the central section of the church was built in the twelfth century after the disastrous fire of 1105 which destroyed most of the original building. Some of the families of fishermen had become secure and wealthy enough to put time and energy into rebuilding it, but in the fourteenth and fifteenth centuries San Nicolo was plagued by earthquakes. Again it was rebuilt, and this time enlarged in the newly-popular Gothic style.

By the end of the sixteenth century various other misfortunes had left the church badly undermined, and a huge wooden beam had to be built across the chancel to steady the walls. The whole nave, including the beam, was decorated with panelling in the Renaissance style and a series of painted wooden statues of Christ, the Apostles and other figures. Above the panelling, pupils of one of the finest of sixteenth-century Venetian painters, Paolo Veronese, painted canvases for the upper part of the walls and the ceiling, the best of which is a centrepiece in the ceiling showing San Nicolo in glory. By 1600, twenty years before the Pilgrim Fathers sailed for America, the church itself was thus in glory too.

When Napoleon arrived to humiliate and wind up the Venetian Republic, San Nicolo was still a thriving religious institution. There were five priests living on the premises, and enough transportable wealth to make it a target for gangs of French looters. During the nineteenth and twentieth centuries it grew damper and dingier. There was a substantial restoration at the turn of the century, but it merely slowed the rate of deterioration. When UNESCO prepared its catalogue of churches, *palazzi* and works of art in need of restoration, San Nicolo emerged as one of the buildings that most urgently required attention.

Immediately after the 1966 floods, Sir Ashley, working with the Italian Art and Archives Fund, had supervised the restoration of the Madonna dell'Orto. By the time it was finished he had acquired considerable experience in restoration, and as a recently retired man he also had spare time. The

Art and Archives Fund was wound up, and another founded
to concentrate specifically on Venice (Venice in Peril). It
wanted a project ambitious enough to absorb a major part of
its resources, but not so ambitious that it would exhaust the
generosity of its British donors. Clarke recalled San Nicolo,
and one of the attractions of the little church off the tourist
track was that it was probably the cheapest project on the
list of urgent cases.

Clarke himself was willing to move to Venice to supervise
the work, and when the two Superintendents, Valcanover
and Padoan, were consulted, they were both enthusiastic,
so much so that Valcanover said that he would pay for the
restoration of the paintings and wooden statues from his own
budget.

The first job at San Nicolo was to restore the structure
itself and make it watertight. So the paintings came down
from the ceiling and the walls, the wooden statues were
taken away for closer scrutiny, and the contractor set to work
on the floor and the roof. Padoan thought that the cost of
fixing the roof, one of the most basic tasks, would be 2
million lire (£1,400), but the first estimate was 14 million
lire (£9,400). It was, like the church, never mind Venice, a
case study of the rule made by the American ecologist Barry
Commoner: 'Once you understand a problem, you find that
it is worse than you expected.' Clarke went off to Padoan
and said that since the error was hardly Venice in Peril's,
could it please have the extra money for the roof from the
Italian government. Padoan took the point, and managed to
secure the extra funds from Rome.

The problem of the floor was less straightforward. One
reason why San Nicolo drew flood water to it was simply
that the heavier the building on the surface of Venice, the

faster it sinks into the lagoon. This is why in many of the older churches the existing floor has been superimposed on an earlier one. Such was the case in San Nicolo; and even the existing floor was below the level of the pavement outside, which meant very heavy pressure of water under the church every time the canals flooded. There was another reason for the flooding. Shortly after work had begun at San Nicolo the council workmen drained the Rio delle Terese for cleaning. Clarke went over to look at the muddy bottom. There he noticed on the side of the canal, a number of holes, relics of the mediaeval drainage system, leading directly under the church. Clarke immediately insisted that they be filled in, despite the workmen's advice that since they had been there for a long time they could not be doing much harm. After the holes were filled the amount of water in the church floor was much less.

San Nicolo was not, of course, the only church in Venice to flood, and Venetian builders had developed specialized methods of dealing with it. Basically, this was to take up the floor and excavate to a depth of some 15 inches. A layer of gravel then went in to defuse the force of the water, spreading it evenly underneath the floor instead of letting it concentrate in vulnerable spots. The gravel would then be covered with concrete, and the tiles replaced. The trouble was that this system did not work very well. The concrete tended to crack under pressure, the water came through the cracks and the cycle of destruction started all over again.

Then one day a New Zealander called Graham Hitchins turned up in Venice. Hitchins, head of a big firm of construction engineers operating mostly in Australia and South-east Asia, had some experience with flooding floors. Indeed, he thought that the problems in the Temple of the Dawn in

Bangkok, which his firm were at the moment damp-proofing and restoring, were remarkably similar to San Nicolo's, so he offered to help.

Hitchins suggested pouring the concrete which would cover the gravel in the floor of San Nicolo into small sections joined to each other by a watertight but slightly flexible sealing compound. This would make the floor as a whole more flexible and the concrete less likely to crack. Hitchens' second innovation was to cover the concrete with a waterproof membrane of resin. When all this was done, and as many of the fifteenth-century tiles as possible replaced, the floor looked rather as it had done before, except that now it was dry, and what had been San Nicolo's most intractable problem had been solved.

The next step was to install a heating system. Quite properly, Clarke discussed with Padoan, the location of the exhaust pipe from the heating boiler since it would affect the church's exterior. They agreed that the best place for it to run would be up the side of the fourteenth-century house that had been built in the gap between the church and its campanile. (That the house should have been built there at all is a reflection on mediaeval town planning.) But when the exhaust pipe was erected the occupants of the house threatened to sue the church, Venice in Peril, Superintendent Padoan, the contractors, and anyone else who had been even marginally involved. The exhaust pipe came down, Clarke and Padoan went back to the drawing board, and the pipe now emerges on the south side of the church's roof.

While the building work was going on, the wooden statues, San Nicolo's proudest possessions, were being restored, mainly by a young German called Max Leuthenmayr, working on Superintendent Valcanover's staff. His

he wanted to lower the height of the altar so that he could celebrate facing the congregation. It was a small job involving a few bricks and some slabs of marble, but no fundamental alteration to the appearance of the church. Nevertheless, it did involve change, and therefore Padoan's formal permission was needed. The priest asked, but got no reply. The office of the Superintendent of Monuments is overstretched and understaffed, and men with too many decisions to make sometimes find it difficult to take any at all. The priest decided, as many Italians had done before him, that the best way to deal with an immobile bureaucracy was to ignore it. He went ahead with the alteration, only to see the bureaucracy suddenly spring to life. Father Scarpa was tried in an administrative court, found guilty and fined 600,000 lire (£400), which is a good deal more than the parish could afford. Rules were there to be observed, said the bureaucrats. Fortunately means were found to suspend the fine, subject to there being no recurrence of the offence, but not before the tolerance of everyone involved had been severely tested.

Another problem was the continual rise in costs. It was not just the roof or the exhaust pipe. An over-enthusiastic Venetian plasterer redecorated one of the side chapels in the ornate, pastel-coloured local manner to a higher standard than the budget allowed. He had to be paid. It was decided at a fairly late stage that the eighteenth-century organ should be restored because it had suffered from damp and neglect during the long years when the church was closed. Clarke succeeded in getting the instrument listed as being of historical importance, so it qualified for a grant from the Italian government. It was sent away for restoration, and the rest of the extra money needed was raised in Britain. The final touch was the carefully-planned lighting, which on feast days gives the restored works of art their full value.

When all the bills were added up, Venice in Peril had spent more than £50,000 on San Nicolo, and the Italian government, by restoring the paintings and statues and paying a share of the roof and the organ, had spent about the same. So the cost was around £100,000, and that took no account of the labour, application and expertise of Clarke and the enthusiasts who helped for nothing at all.

But thanks to their money and effort San Nicolo dei Mendicoli is now unlike any other church in Venice: its art and architecture exhibit a total catholicity of style and material. It is intimate, and friendly, spruce and cluttered at the same time, and full of thoughtful detail, like the red drapes on the pillars which highlight the decorations on the capitals during feast days. It is not a church to go to for a particularly great Titian or Tintoretto (though the large polychrome wooden statue of the patron saint has emerged as one of the most important Gothic sculptures in the city). It is a fine example of what, after twelve centuries of mixed fortunes in a remarkable environment, a Venetian church can look like without being transformed into a museum. Indeed, one of the better compliments to Venice in Peril comes from Father Scarpa. He reports, with a vast contented smile, that attendances at Mass are up.

CHAPTER 11

Deadline 1989

When Sir John Pope-Hennessy, then director of the Victoria and Albert Museum, realized how badly the stone statues in Florence had been damaged in the 1966 floods, he immediately sent for his chief stone restorer, Kenneth Hempel, and suggested that he go to Italy and see what he could do. In Florence Hempel was first asked how the statues could be returned to the exact condition in which they had been before the flood. The flood water had removed the surface dirt, and the general opinion was that the statues looked too clean without their patina. Hempel, for his part, had a rare chance to see just how much decay had been camouflaged by the dirt. He reported back to Pope-Hennessy that if the statues were returned to their previous condition they would continue to decay. If they were to be saved, they would have to be cleaned and conserved.

Pope-Hennessy told him to get on with it, concluding that this was the single area in which the Victoria and Albert might make its most significant contribution to preserving Italian art. Having got the job, Hempel set about finding out how best to tackle it, not only in Florence, but elsewhere in Italy, and on his first visit to Venice was alarmed to discover that its stone too was in appalling condition—in fact far worse than Florence. (One stone restorer he met commented: 'They should have started worrying about Venice in 1910.')

The UNESCO-financed survey of the condition of Venetian stone carried out after the 1966 flood confirmed Hempel's visual impression: 35 per cent of the *patrimonio artistico*— which embraces all buildings and statues—was already in a state of grave deterioration. Moreover, the annual rate of loss of stone work was between 4 and 6 per cent a year. At that rate it would all have crumbled away by 1989.

Worse, there was disagreement among the small body of international experts about the best method of saving stone —the literature on the subject is so thin that it can be carried away from a library under one arm—and because there was no way of cleaning and conserving that was one hundred per cent safe many stone experts counselled caution. The experts meet irregularly in Bologna, and at the first of their conferences in 1969 Hempel made it perfectly clear where he stood: 'I think it would be a mistake to be too careful. If we are, the result will be that we will do nothing, and the monuments will have fallen to pieces and be lost.'

Hempel had already begun to search for a proper diagnosis. The first thing to discover was whether the problem was particularly Venetian. It took only a short trip to mainland towns like Vicenza and Verona to settle that one: the same architects had used the same stone, and it was in much better shape than the stone in Venice. The next step was to try to discover the reason for Venetian decay, and the newness of this work meant that theories were plentiful.

The French, for example, were particularly enamoured of the idea that the deterioration of stone was caused by bacteria. It is quite true that each piece of decayed stone observed under a microscope did contain bacteria, and Hempel took the possibility seriously enough when he began his work in Venice in 1967. He and the chief chemist at the Victoria and Albert Museum, Anne Moncrief, eliminated it by subjecting the theory to comparative analysis. If bacteria were destroying the stone of Venice they should be destroying stone in Yugoslavia, not far away down the Adriatic coast, in old towns not unlike Venice where people lived cheek by jowl in sanitary conditions which still left much to be desired, and obviously allowed bacteria to flourish. But there was no decay there. If bacteria were responsible in Venice, it was clearly a unique variety of bug that was at work.

The theory could not withstand observation and common sense, never mind scientific analysis. Hempel, a believer in the virtues of observation and common sense, refers to what he describes in the theology of stone restoration as 'the Parable of the Concrete Yard'. If a yard is covered with virgin concrete there are no living organisms growing in the concrete; it is stone. But as it weathers, the frost cracks it, and the rain enlarges the cracks. They grow large enough to allow particles of dust to settle, and, when there is soil, seeds germinate, and when the plants grow they open the cracks. 'You can't have a rookery until you've got rooks,' says Hempel. 'And you can't have bacterial action on stone until it has broken up.'

A second theory, which had been the subject of a paper in the very first international conference on stone preservation, held in 1967 in Brussels, had proposed salt water as the culprit; and there is no shortage of salt water in Venice. So Hempel conducted a simple experiment at the Victoria and Albert. He placed a piece of marble half in and half out of a salt solution for three weeks. During this time the salt solution permeated the marble and crept into the dry half.

But when Hempel examined it, the stone which had remained immersed in the salt solution had not been affected
at all. The only deterioration was in the marble above the
surface, permeated by the salt solution, and open to the
atmosphere. The conclusion was that the decay was not
caused by the salt itself. It occurred because of the crystalliza-
tion of the salt in the open air. When the water evaporated,
the crystals of salt created pressure on the marble surface and
began to break it up, in much the same way as frost might.
The action was mechanical, not chemical.

Hempel's Venice trips had alerted him to another, very
particularly Venetian theory. Venice had thousands of
pigeons, especially in St Mark's Square, all depositing their
excrement in vast quantities on the stone of the city. Perhaps
they were the cause; it was a popular theory, but untested.
In a mild parody of scientific prose, Hempel explained to the
Bologna conference of stone experts in October 1971 how
he went about investigating its validity.

Two rock pigeons were confined in a pigeon loft constructed in such a manner that all their droppings would
fall upon selected stone samples. This loft was positioned
on the roof of the Victoria and Albert Museum. Their
diet was arranged to be commensurate with that commonly consumed by pigeons in cities—mixed corn, black
peas and occasionally bread. Their kind, attracted by the
food, were able to communicate with them through the
bars of the loft, which prevented the possibility of isola-
tion from virus or parasites which might have had an
influence on the result.

Prior to the introduction of the stone samples, and after
allowing the birds to settle in, a measurement of their

daily droppings was made. It was found that a bird averaged a daily (24 hours) waste of 12 grammes. A quick calculation leaves one wondering why San Marco has not disappeared beneath pigeon droppings. Luckily much of the 12 grammes is water, which evaporates and, of the solids, much is washed away by rain. It is in the sheltered and semi-sheltered conditions that droppings build up upon the architecture and sculpture. Our experiment was designed to reproduce just these conditions.

Hempel chose three kinds of stone for the experiment, Carrara and Greek marble and Istrian stone, and the surface of each was polished so that it would register change quickly. They were then oven-dried and weighed on bullion scales in Hatton Garden, the diamond quarter of London.

The samples were introduced to the pigeon loft in November and for a time had to be carefully changed in position to enable them to be equally fouled. This finally became unnecessary as the birds themselves changed their roosts. For the first couple of months the samples were alternatively wet or dry in accordance with the weather. Some freezing took place, but no very low temperatures were recorded in London in the winter of 1970–71. As time went on the build-up of droppings cemented the samples to the floor and the frequent drying ceased. Round the edges of the stone waste grain germinated but died after growing an inch or so either as a result of frost, damping or being pecked and trodden on.

The stone stayed there for six months before it was taken back to the laboratory, hosed down, and oven-dried once more. The conclusions were as follows:

In all three cases the tell-tale polish was only slightly affected, and even this deterioration was very irregular. The Carrara and Greek marbles were slightly stained. Little alteration in colour could be detected on the Istrian. If we relate these results to an earlier experiment in which a piece of Carrara fully exposed but without the influence of pigeons lost its polish in two months upon the Museum roof, and that in the relatively salubrious autumnal weather, we must draw only one conclusion: the pigeon droppings had masked the stone from its main enemy, the atmosphere.

Hempel was convinced by now that he would find the reason for the destruction of Venetian stone in the atmosphere, and that the answer when it came would be expressed in chemical terms. There was already growing evidence that a combination of sulphur dioxide (SO_2) and water (H_2O) harmed stone. Venice had no shortage of either. The water came not just in the form of rain, but in sea spray during the bad storms, and as humidity—and Venice is unusually humid at most times of year. But water alone could not destroy the stone: if it could, Venice would have disappeared centuries ago.

What happened in the twentieth century was that water combined with sulphur dioxide, setting off a particular chemical reaction for the first time. This operated with such ferocity that inestimable amounts of damage were done before anyone knew how to deal with it.

Sulphur dioxide is given off when fossil fuels are burned, so any industrial society must have been filling the air with SO_2 for years now. When water and sulphur dioxide mix, they become sulphuric acid. Sulphuric acid (H_2SO_4)

combines with calcium carbonate (Ca) in the stone and this in turn becomes calcium sulphate ($CaSO_4$). Calcium sulphate is larger in volume than the calcium carbonate of the stone. As Hempel explains, the effect is explosive: 'The stone is literally blown to bits.'

Hempel was not the only man working towards this conclusion, and there was useful confirmation of it in the papers prepared by the International Centre for Conservation and Restoration in Rome, which was being partly financed by UNESCO after 1967. The first analysis of the chemical causes of stone decay was delivered by the Centre's director, Giorgio Torraca, at the earliest Bologna conference in 1969, and he illustrates the process with a set of pictures of stone, each magnified 500 times. These showed the fibres which make up the stone, tightly knit at first, bursting apart under the pressure of calcium sulphate.

What happens next can be observed by the naked eye. The calcium sulphate, infecting the stone like a malignant tumour, mixes with soot in the atmosphere, and the surface of the stone is transformed into gypsum, or crumbled stone. Often the black encrustation hides what is going on underneath, but the merest touch will bring the surface away entirely. In terms of art rather than science, it means that the decoration on the stone disappears into dust.

Once the process of destruction begun by sulphur dioxide is under way, other elements—some of which had earlier been thought of as the main cause of destruction—attack the stone. Crystallized salt from the sea spray and the wash of canal boats cause the stone to break up further. It is now possible for bacteria to multiply. If the extent of damage could be plotted on a graph, the speed of destruction would have to be shown on a logarithmic scale, starting very gradually and eventually ascending so steeply as to become a straight line.

By the 1970s Hempel and Torraca had learned enough about the subject to know how tardy their discovery had been. 'In a way,' said Torraca later, 'we were already too late from a sculptural point of view. All the fine detail had been lost. Architecturally, though, there was still time to save something.' That, however, involved controls on industry, for the major source of sulphur dioxide in the air over Venice came from Porto Marghera and Mestre.

Measurements began in 1972. The presence of sulphur dioxide in the atmosphere is described in parts per million. Italian law allows 0.30 parts per million. In 1973, during a study period lasting fifteen weeks, Porto Marghera exceeded the limit on an average of once a week. True, a comparison showed that the level in Venice was similar to that in central London on a winter day, but most London building stone is 300 years younger than that of Venice.

The point was that because there remained scientific debate about the danger of sulphur dioxide, even 0.30 parts per million could be too high (Sweden, for example, has much stricter limits). Yet the doubt allowed the Porto Marghera industrialists to argue for minimum safeguards. Their opponents, usually laymen who were much less well organized and financed, argued that the solution was to move Porto Marghera up the coast towards Trieste, as though the petro-chemical factories were cards in a game of industrial Monopoly. These extreme claims helped big business because they alienated the trade unions, which were reluctant to support plans that would put their members out of work.

The outcome of the wrangle was a compromise. Monte-dison budgeted for an astonishing 30 billion lire (£20 million) for pollution controls, though not much of that had been allocated by the mid-1970s, partly out of lack of enthusiasm for such spending, and partly because of the difficulty in getting planning permission out of the Venice government. Between 1972 and 1973 British Petroleum, which had a four million ton refinery in Mestre, spent 3 billion lire building a higher chimney and improving the quality of water being returned to the lagoon. This sounded fine, except there is evidence that it was all too late.

Hempel and Anne Moncrief began to relate their chemical conclusions to historical evidence. They wanted to know why Venetian stone had only just begun to deteriorate. Sulphur dioxide from the burning of coal had been around long enough to have had some impact on stone, and yet serious damage had been noticed only a few years earlier. There are photographs of the statues on the façade of St Mark's Cathedral taken in the 1930s which showed the ancient stone in almost perfect condition. Yet only thirty years later it had started to fall apart, and after another ten years it was in an advanced state of decay.

The two experts went back over the process of deterioration. The first stage is the thermal shock, which starts the day the stone is quarried. Next comes the erosion by wind and rain; after that, the activity of frost, when water freezes in minute cracks and breaks up the surface of the stone. The impact of sulphur dioxide comes at the fourth stage, and Hempel and Moncrief began to wonder whether it mattered at all how much sulphur dioxide there was; whether it might not be a catalyst which would destroy, no matter how little there was in the air. This suggested that even if the petrochemical complex in Porto Marghera was shut down completely, and no one in Venice burned oil for domestic heating, there would still be enough sulphur dioxide in the air to trigger the process of destruction. Hempel is matter of fact about it. 'With Marghera as it is now, you still have quite enough SO_2 to do enormous damage. In fact, if you closed the lot down tomorrow the process of decay would continue.'

Earlier, Hempel had concluded that the battle should be fought on two fronts: the first was to identify the source of the sulphur dioxide which was destroying the stone; that had been done but the solution was not in his province. So there remained only a single front: the search for a satisfactory way of cleaning the stone and conserving it—making it impervious to the poisoned atmosphere that surrounded it.

When Hempel first went to Italy he had already invented a method of cleaning statues which involved mixing deionized water with fine earth, and plastering the statues with a mixture not unlike a mud pack. The principle was much the same: the mixture dissolved the sulphuration on the statue and drew it out of the stone and into the mud, leaving the stone free of destructive chemicals. He decided to try this method in Venice. The statue he chose was a Virgin and Child above the central door of the church of the Miracoli. The mud was mixed and placed on the statue but it failed. The encrustation of sulphuration was too thick to yield to the cleaner.

Hempel started at the beginning again. The obvious way to clean things, surely, was with water. A layman might reasonably propose soap and water, but the calcium carbonate of the stone combines with soap to create a water-resistant film which picks up dirt. Another is wire brushes, but brushing might damage the surface of the stone, and tiny fragments of wire would remain behind. The wire then acts as a catalyst with sulphurous pollution, accelerating the damage it can cause. Hempel looked at industrial methods. The most commonly used is sand blasting, which uses the abrasive properties of sand multiplied by compressed air. But it was at best a clumsy method, often cutting away the stone it was cleaning, and entirely lacking the precision which Hempel needed for works of art. Chemical cleaning was too drastic. 'Any acid, from a lemon upward, will etch marble. Just put it on and watch it fizz,' says Hempel. 'But what disappears is not just the polluted encrustation but the stone too.'

So Hempel turned to the abrasive technique, and sought ways of refining it. Ultrasonic dental cleaning equipment might work. So Hempel decided to try it on the face of St Christopher, high on the façade of the Madonna dell'Orto. The dirt which had stained St Christopher's cheeks like black tears was cleaned away without damaging the stone underneath at all. The trouble was that the scale was too small. The abrasive process had been designed for human teeth, not stone faces. Hempel looked around Venice, considered the extent of stone damage, and realized that with a dentist's drill the task would take decades.

In 1971 Hempel took time off from Italy and went to the Smithsonian Museum in Washington DC. One of the experts there, Bethune Gibson, was cleaning American Indian buckskins and pottery, which were even more fragile than Venetian marble; she was using an air abrasion machine made to cut quartz into small enough pieces to put in watches. It was also delicate enough to clean as well as cut, as long as it was used properly. Hempel learnt that the quartz cutter was made under licence by an English company, GEC-Elliott, in the London suburb of Lewisham. He went there with a piece of stone, asked if he could fiddle about with the machine for a while—and the result was better than anything he had done before. Instead of sand, the abrasive material was tiny glass beads, so small that they felt like silk; and unlike sand they did not cut into the stone at all. Hempel was delighted: 'It worked like a dream.'

Hempel now began to look for a method of preserving stone after it had been cleaned. He concluded that most existing methods had done more harm than good. He was worried about the example of the Ca' d'Oro, once the most glamorous of the Grand Canal palaces, since it was not only decorated with marble, but, as its name suggests, with gold too. The gold had gone long ago, and to preserve the marble the restorers had used a simple silicone process to harden the stone. The result was, Hempel observed succinctly, 'disastrous'.

He had been involved in one laborious conservation experiment which had been fairly successful. It was based on solvent known as 'water white, heat-cured, epoxy resin', but the trouble was that it could be applied only when the stone had been dried completely, brought up to a temperature of between 72 and 80 degrees centigrade and kept there for sixteen hours. The difficulties of this system, on the large exterior stone surfaces of Venice, were obvious.

Next Hempel tried a new silicone sample he had picked up in Venice, mixed with water (previously he had used it undiluted). He applied this to a marble piece, and put it on the roof of the Victoria and Albert, with an untreated piece at its side. The results were remarkable.

At the Bologna conference in 1971, Hempel reported enthusiastically: 'Another winter's weathering has only confirmed the phenomenal properties of this material. The original piece of deteriorated marble is showing no signs of breakdown, whereas the untreated sample has deteriorated to a pile of dust.'

When Sir John Pope-Hennessy sent Hempel to Italy, his assignment was not only to find the most satisfactory method of cleaning and restoration. He was also told to search out Italians who could be trained to do the job themselves. There was one man in Florence who had learned the trade under Hempel's guidance at the Victoria and Albert, and he had gone back and done well, but there were few like him. In Venice, in fact, the only one person with the necessary qualities of interest, patience and determination was an Italian girl, Giulia Musumeci. She had worked on the statue of St Christopher at the Madonna dell'Orto and on the Virgin and Child at the Miracoli, but the first great work for which Hempel had found the right stone cleaner, and thought he had the right conserver, was Sansovino's Loggetta at the Campanile, a perfect challenge for a stone restorer. There were different types of marble, pale Carrara and ruddy terracotta-coloured Verona marble, and Istrian stone. There were many finely carved figures, and much decorative detail, all of which had attracted dirt; and behind the encrustation the sulphurous substances were destroying the stone. It was a suitable symbol for the destruction of Venetian stone—highly visible, and terribly vulnerable. Musumeci began work on it in 1972.

A scaffold had to be constructed so that she could place the cleaner, the quartz cutter, at three levels, convenient for her and strong enough to support the machinery. The scaffold was encased in wood, partly to give her privacy, and partly to keep her warm during the cold Venetian winter. But even when the *scirocco* was blowing from the Sahara it was still chilly, and even with a generous-looking scaffolding it was still cramped. Polythene was used to control dust, while cables provided lighting and power for the machine. It was not an atmosphere in which many people would choose to work. The dust made it mandatory to wear a mask, and because the ground glass crystals had to reach every part of the stone, Giulia Musumeci often had to crouch for extended periods of time. If one small area was missed it would not absorb the conserver, and much of the value of the restoration could be lost.

It was a remarkable process to watch. The abrasive glass beads were shot through a pen-like nozzle. If the dirt was thick, the nozzle would be placed near the stone surface, then withdrawn a bit when the encrustation thinned out. One moment there was a square inch of black dirt, and the next it would be clean, white or red again, quite transformed. It took three years to complete the job; first one half of the Loggetta was scaffolded and then the other.

For much of the time, Giulia Musumeci's salary was paid by Venice in Peril—she was eventually employed by the Ministry of Fine Arts. (VIP also met the cost of the scaffold and the cleaning materials.) For brief periods Miss Musumeci had assistants; but none found the job as absorbing as she did herself, and none of them stayed. It was lonely work, but when the Loggetta was formally unveiled again by the Mayor of Venice in September 1974, it had obviously been well worth while. It showed everyone who visited the Piazzetta what could be done in Venice, and how fine the city would look once it had been done. It also demonstrated how long it would take, and what a desperate shortage of

manpower, or womanpower, there was. Hempel, and a few
other experts in the infant field of stone restoring, had dis-
covered how the job could be done, but they had not dis-
covered enough people to do it.

The manpower problem had been known for years to the
Superintendents, and to the funds who were paying for
restoration work. Among the resolutions at a meeting of all
the voluntary funds in 1974 was the following:

> Having examined the problem of conservation and restora-
> tion of stone, we recognize the necessity of creating an
> appropriate laboratory which would also provide profes-
> sional training; and we declare our readiness to carry the
> expenses of running the laboratory for a period to be
> established, but from three to five years, it being under-
> stood that either the Italian state or other public institu-
> tions would provide the necessary building to house it.

That sounds like a simple, generous and sensible proposal; it
was surprising, in fact, that the private funds had waited until
December 1973 to make it. But it was not the first time they
had made the suggestion. If their enthusiasm was tinged with
anxiety, it was because their request that December was the
fourth of its kind, so in the summer of 1974 Sir Ashley
Clarke, hoping to speed things up, wrote a paper on stone
restoration for UNESCO's International Consultative Committee, and after its appearance it seemed as though no one
could possibly fault the proposals on the basis that they had
been insufficiently thought through: Sir Ashley's paper even
contained a detailed organization chart showing who would
do what, and to whom they would be responsible. The
fundamental problem was the absence of a strong pressure
group to force the issue, a point Sir Ashley stressed: 'One of

the greatest obstacles to the formation of a body of expert stone restorers is the fact that there is no proper career structure available to those who acquire the necessary skills. Consequently recruitment of suitable personnel is extremely difficult.'

So, after eight years' research and experiment by men like Hempel and Torraca, the problem of stone in Venice, the most comprehensive work of architectural art in the world, was no longer a scientific problem; it was known what caused the stone to decay. Nor was it a technical problem; it was known how to clean and conserve stone. It was a personnel problem. Hempel had a characteristically abrasive summary of the position. 'What is the situation at the moment? I'll tell you. There is just one girl working away; God knows how she sticks it. It's absolutely bloody hopeless.'

CHAPTER 12

A Way but no Will

THE disaster of 1966 made it clear to everyone interested in saving Venice that the lagoon was at the heart of the matter. Every problem the city faced—flooding, subsidence, brick and stone decay, pollution—either began with the lagoon or was somehow involved with it. Individuals and voluntary groups were able to help with restoration but, admirable though this work might be, it would turn out to be a waste of time and money unless something was done about the lagoon. The job was too big for any voluntary body to tackle. The costs, skills, and political push needed could come only from the Italian government.

At the beginning it appeared that the government realized this, and was prepared to accept the responsibility. In 1969 it set up the Institute for the Study of the Dynamics of Grand Masses specifically to look at the problems of the lagoon. The institute was given a home in a fine sixteenth-century *palazzo* on the Grand Canal, the Palazzo Papadopoli, and a bright and dedicated scientist, Roberto Frassetto, appointed as director. Although when Frassetto arrived to take up his duties there was no staff, no furniture, no laboratory and no instruments, there was a fund of goodwill, not only in Venice but internationally. That this was so, became evident when René Maheu arrived in Venice from UNESCO headquarters and called on Frassetto out of curiosity. He looked over the empty Palazzo, listened to Frassetto's plans and finally said, 'I'm impressed. I like your approach. What do you need?' 'Tools and brains,' Frassetto said. 'Let me know when you need them,' Maheu replied.

Over the next five years, seventy-five scientists from all over the world visited Frassetto and the young, inexperienced staff working with him in Venice. 'We'd have a problem,' Frassetto recalls. 'I'd think who was the best man in that field. I'd ring him in, say Australia, and ask him if he could come to see us for a long week-end. If he agreed, UNESCO would pay his fare, and we'd look after him here. There was never any question of fees. They did it for science, and for Venice.'

The absence of tools was solved in much the same way. Some were not available in Italy, and, even if they were, the bureaucratic delays in getting the most important of them would have been intolerable, so many were borrowed, usually from abroad.

For example, Britain's National Institute of Oceanography lent Frassetto two instruments. One, a gauge to measure fluctuations in water levels, was the first of its kind in the world, and the NIO was anxious to see how it would perform mounted in a large buoy moored in mid-ocean. The other instrument was an electro-magnetic sea current meter which was mounted on an oceanographic tower ten miles offshore from the Lido, where it measured wave speeds and gave valuable information about wave directions and currents.

Although these results were for Frassetto's own use, the problems they could help solve were remarkably similar to some in Britain. London is sinking, relative to the Thames, at about the same rate as Venice, and South East England, including London, is liable to severe flooding from storm surges generated in the shallow North Sea. As UNESCO says: 'As a physical environmental problem, Venice is an excellent model for research. This city is affected by the majority of the ill effects of the physical environment which threatens the northern cities of the world.'

Frassetto, too, realized the wider implications of his work in Venice. The first dimension was obvious: it was to investigate the mechanism of Venice's floods, subsidence and pollution. The second conformed to his basic scientific objective, 'to provide a public service, because this is the only way that education and research can achieve something useful for everybody.' This is an attractive trait, and it was Frassetto's enthusiasm, as much as Venice itself, that brought him help from his international colleagues and UNESCO.

Frassetto is a figure out of a romantic novel. Born in Capri of Sardinian and French parents, he became a war hero, taking part in one of the most daring naval raids of the Second World War. When a group of Italian frogmen attacked British vessels in Alexandria harbour on 18 December 1941, Frassetto was one of the 'human torpedoes'. He survived and, after seeing the war out in prisoner of war camps, returned home to find himself the recipient of the Medallio d'Oro, the equivalent of the vc, or the Congressional Medal of Honour.

He had studied engineering at Florence before the war, and he now completed his education as an oceanographer, at Yale and Columbia. He was fascinated by the aberrant behaviour of the sea, and before moving to Venice he had completed distinguished undersea research work in the Mediterranean and was head of the oceanography section of the Italian National Research Council (CNR).

His flaw—or strength, perhaps—seemed to be a considerable impatience with the compromises made and demanded
by politicians. Frassetto believes that a scientific truth is a
scientific truth, and that no amount of bending can change it.
Not that this made him any less a practical figure. He never
entertained, for example, any hope that Venice's problems
might be solved by moving Marghera away from the lagoon.
On the contrary, he accepts the Chamber of Commerce
vision of Venice as the second Italian port after Genoa. Nor
does he sentimentalize the future, by proposing, for instance,
a reduction in the amount of boat traffic on the canals: 'We
cannot pretend that the *vaporetti* will disappear, and the gondola will come back. That would be living in a fantasy world.'

Frassetto's first task was eased by the assistance of the most
important single instrument which had been placed at his
disposal. This was the computer at the IBM study centre in
Venice, and he used it to construct a mathematical model of
the lagoon and the surrounding area. 'In the old days, we'd
have used 10,000 slaves and tackled the problems on a trial
and error basis,' Frassetto says. He continues:

We can't do that now. We construct a computer model
instead. Once we have a simulation of the real thing we
can then change the input any way we want to and we can
see what happens. The behaviour of the water in the lagoon
is governed by well-established hydraulic laws, so we can
learn in advance how successful any modification is likely
to be.

We measure water speed, its level, the atmospheric
pressure, wind speed, and direction, then feed this information into the mathematical model on the computer. It
then tells us what will happen next on the lagoon at

virtually any point. A simple example: if we feed in the measurements taken by instruments at the mouth of the Lido entrance the computer immediately tells us what the behaviour of the water will be when it reaches Punta Salute, five miles away.

The calculations are very complex. The equations involve over a thousand factors and each of the quantities we are examining has specific and different values. There is an enormous volume of calculations involved, and only a computer can handle them.

The data for these calculations came from mareographic stations in the lagoon, from the institute's platform in the Adriatic off the Lido, and from a second platform belonging to the Institute for Marine Engineering of Padua University, sited off the Malamocco outlet. (Plans call for the linking of all this equipment direct to the computer so that information would be coming in continuously and virtually instantaneously.)

Constructing the mathematical model involved a new study of the phenomenon of the *acque alte*. Some of the factors that contribute to these were already well-known. The physical laws of a natural high tide, for example, were clearly understood and did not present any problem of forecasting or calculation. But this tide, by itself insufficient to flood Venice, is on occasions boosted by two other factors. One is the south-easterly wind or *scirocco*, which pushes the Adriatic up towards Venice when a storm affects the Italian peninsula. The other is a system of free wave patterns on the whole Adriatic after a storm. These patterns continue with a momentum of their own even when the storm has gone. They begin near Otranto at the entrance to the Adriatic, and cause a rise in the level of the sea which steadily increases until it reaches its maximum at Venice.

Eventually, the researchers at the Palazzo Papadopoli evolved a way of predicting when any combination of factors would cause flooding in Venice. This prediction required feeding the computer information on sea levels, meteorological descriptions of new storms over the Adriatic and calculations for the normal tide. The basic principle was that if in the past floods occurred when these factors were at certain levels or combinations, then the same cause and effect relationship would hold good in the future.

Over four years records were built up on which to base predictions, and the mathematical model put into action. As a routine measure, Italian meteorological stations report every three hours to the Air Force Meteorological Service in Rome, from where reports are retransmitted to all airports. When a storm was forecast, the Venice airport telephoned the Palazzo Papadopoli, where the information was fed into the flood forecast model. The computer compared the new data with its historical records and announced whether conditions favourable to flooding existed. If they did, then the Tides Forecast Office was alerted and it sounded sirens to warn Venice. The first test came on 5 January 1968, when the Institute was able to predict an *acqua alta* with remarkable precision. By 1975, during the serious November floods, it was able to give as much as six hours' warning.

The second problem to which Frassetto addressed himself was subsidence. A special drill extracted a core 4 inches in diameter and 3,250 feet long from the earth under Venice. It was one of the longest continuous cores extracted anywhere in the world, and was studied not only in Venice, but at Manchester University's Department of Soil Mechanics as well. During this investigation Frassetto drew a profile of Venice to see if there had been any pattern to the subsidence. To his alarm, the profile revealed a secondary result of the city's sinking. In some sections the subsidence had so disturbed foundations that the buildings had started to slip sideways into the canals.

On a visit to the United States, Frassetto came across a technique for lifting buildings called mud-jacking, and realized immediately that it could be used in Venice. The principle is straightforward. A neutral substance—mud is ideal—is injected under pressure into holes drilled in the ground surrounding the building to be lifted. The mud infiltrates the subsoil, swelling it upwards at a controllable rate. Depending on the pressure and the spacing of the injections, the distance the building is lifted can be as delicate as a tenth of an inch a year or as much as four inches in six months. Again, depending on the location of the holes for the injection, all the ground can be raised, or only part of it, so as to level out an incline. Experienced American mud-jackers told Frassetto that they were confident that they could not only raise and stabilize buildings slipping into Venice's canals, but they could even straighten the leaning tower of Pisa.

But, Frassetto reasoned, a stabilized building is not saved, only reprieved. If its brickwork continues to be soaked with salt water and continues to crumble, its destruction will be as certain as if it were allowed to slip into the canal. So he began to look for a system that would consolidate the brickwork and make it waterproof. He examined a British technique developed to combat a frequently encountered weakness in Victorian-built housing, rising damp. A silicone-based liquid is introduced into the brickwork through a series of holes

A Way but no Will

drilled into the wall. Like water, the silicone creeps throughout the bricks' structure by capillary action, and once it is dry
it renders the brickwork impervious to moisture.

The more Frassetto examined the difficulties of subsidence,
decay and instability in Venice, the more certain he was that
the overriding problem was the flooding, and that the answer
was not simply to *predict* the *acque alte* but to *control* them;
and that meant cutting the lagoon off from the Adriatic. The
obvious way to do this was to dam the three entrances, the
Lido, Malamocco, and Chioggia channels. Venice would
then sit safely in a tideless lagoon, protected from the sea
forever. But such a course was totally out of the question. To
begin with, the port of Venice would be finished. Without
its shipping, the Porto Marghera industrial complex would
wither. This would be economically and politically un-
acceptable, and incompatible with Frassetto's search for a
solution for Venice that was compatible with progress.

Moreover, the lagoon itself, shut off from the sea, would
die. Since Venice has no sewage system and its waste empties
untreated into its canals, the ebb and flow of the tides from
the Adriatic are essential to keep the lagoon fresh. And even
if a sewage plant were built, there would still remain the
problem of the chemical discharges from industry. If these,
too, could be eliminated, there would still be the destruction
of marine life when the water changed from salt to fresh, as
evaporation was replenished from the rivers emptying into
the lagoon. Clearly, permanent closure was out, so Frassetto
examined instead the logical alternative: temporary closure
of the three entrances when the computer predicted danger
of flooding.

In 1970 the Institute sponsored a competition, inviting
suggestions for a system that would allow the lagoon to be

closed when necessary. The conditions were that the device should allow free passage for ships when open, should be able to block the entrances quickly when flooding threatened and should be technically and financially feasible.

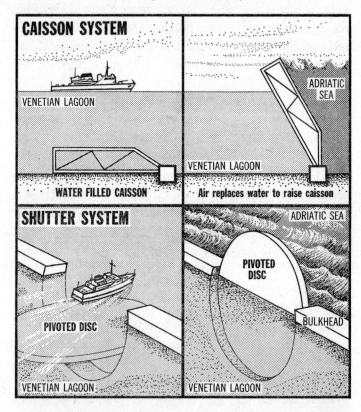

The competition produced a variety of solutions: a giant caisson, hinged at one end, designed to lie flat on the seabed when filled with water but to swing upright on the hinge when filled with air; a pivoted disc, that would be underwater when horizontal but would block the entrance when pivoted to a vertical position; and a series of locks and sluice gates not dissimilar to those on the Panama Canal. All the systems were feasible. The question was which would work best, and which would cost least. The Lido channel is nearly five-eighths of a mile wide and would need as many as forty gates—expensive to install, operate and maintain. None the less, Frassetto was now confident that an engineering solution for the lagoon was entirely possible, and he proposed to follow this competition with a feasibility and cost study. In 1971 he estimated that the study would need $500,000 and take six months. The politicians who had to provide the money were not enthusiastic, and the study did not take place.

By the summer of 1975 the only indication that anyone outside the Institute cared enough to do something about the lagoon entrances came from private enterprise. A consortium comprising Pirelli, the Italian rubber company, Erika Glanzstoff, a man-made fibre group, and Furlanis, a construction firm, proposed a new scheme which had the advantage of low initial cost, and a short installation period. Their system consisted of a long flexible tube, or bag, made of nylon coated with synthetic rubber. One of these would span each of the lagoon openings, and be held in place by cables running from each side of the tube to concrete pylons driven into the seabed. When deflated, the tube would lie flat and out of sight deep under water. When flooding threatened, pumping stations would fill the tube with sea water. The inflated tube would then rise and block the entrance. When the danger had passed, the pumping stations would pump out the water and the tube would sink again to the seabed. The rubber gates offered the advantage of flexibility, absorbing instead of reflecting the force of waves beating against them. They would not detract from the landscape, or disturb any of the natural balances of the

£14.22 million. UNESCO immediately offered to guarantee a credit to help finance the whole operation.

Frassetto preferred the design for steel gates submitted for the Institute's competition in 1970, but he did not want to be dogmatic about it, and thought that a combination of rubber and steel gates might well work. The main thing, he felt, was the interest stirred by the intensive public relations campaign which accompanied the Pirelli experiment, and UNESCO's offer to guarantee credit would get things moving.

Instead, Pirelli's experiment served as a reminder of how much money could be at stake in saving Venice. It seemed to whet appetites and revive factions. The scheme was said to be pushed by the rubber lobby in Rome, and met with bitter opposition from the representatives of the cement lobby, supporting a more traditional system which would, naturally, use more cement. But by this time the problem of the lagoon entrances had not only created commercial rivalry; it had become hopelessly enmeshed in the Rome bureaucracy, and this was infinitely more serious.

The general administration of the Special Law for Venice which provided for the gates came under the Director-General of Public Works. He was advised on specialist and technical matters by a Grand Committee, which divided into sub-committees to deal with various aspects of the Venice problem. The fourth sub-committee was the one appointed to consider the best way of protecting Venice from floods. It deliberated throughout the autumn and winter of 1973–74 and, on a majority vote, came out in favour of Frassetto's 'mobile closure system' of steel gates to shut out the sea from the lagoon.

But the Grand Committee was concerned that the fourth

sub-committee's decision had not been unanimous, that the divisions within the sub-committee were deep, and that its conclusions had not been 'real and practical', so it rejected the recommendation and ordered the fourth sub-committee to think again. But, with one of those bewildering twists not uncommon in Rome, before the sub-committee could get around to reconsidering the matter, the Grand Committee itself was dissolved. A new committee, the Senior Council of the Public Works Ministry, started on the problem from scratch with orders to report before the end of March 1975.

Frassetto and UNESCO were asked for their views and spent considerable time preparing a report recommending the mobile closure system. In the first week of March, Frassetto travelled to Rome to present this report at a meeting of the Public Works Senior Council. There, to his amazement, he found that the Council had already made its decision at its previous meeting.

On 27 March it was publicly announced that the Council had recommended, and the Ministry had agreed, that, in order to 'preserve the hydro-geological balance of the lagoon and to effect a lowering of the *acque alte* in the historic centres to a level at which they will not disturb the functioning of the port and the life of the people, a *fixed system* must be devised which will allow better control of the lagoon openings.' The phrase *fixed system* ruled out not only the Pirelli scheme, but every other idea submitted for Frassetto's 1970 competition.

The decision appeared final, but there was one chance of changing it. At the same time as it announced the Council's findings, the Ministry also announced an international competition 'for a contract for the preservation of the hydro-geological equilibrium of the lagoon and for the lowering of the high water levels in the historic centres.' So the Council's conclusion was still only a recommendation, and if an attractive alternative scheme emerged from the international competition then it would stand at least a chance of being adopted.

It was not until September 1975 that details of the competition were announced in the *Gazzetta Ufficiale della Republica Italiana* and, even though it was to be an *international* competition, many months before details were available abroad. Early in 1976 enquirers at the Italian Consulate in London were told that no one knew anything about the competition and were advised to contact the Ministry of Public Works in Rome. There enquirers were referred back to the Italian Consulate in London, where, the Ministry said, English translations of the terms of the competition should be available.

But much more worrying than this buck-passing—which is, after all a bureaucratic technique not confined to Italy—were the conditions of the competition. After stating that the competitors would be given absolute discretion on the nature of the scheme, the official notice then added 'subject to compliance with the terms established in the guidelines laid down by the Government on 27 March 1975.'

The most important guideline states unequivocally:

The hydro-geological equilibrium of the lagoon is to be preserved and high water levels in the historic centres are to be lowered—without exceeding limits to an extent affecting the functioning of the port system and the conduct of normal public activities—by means of a system of *fixed water intake regulating structures*; at a subsequent time, this may be supplemented by mobile structures, if it becomes necessary, due to tide levels, to close the intakes altogether [authors' italics].

Further on, the official announcement says that the Public Works Authority reserves the right to contract solely for the fixed structure 'during the preliminary phase', but if it decided in a later phase to add mobile gates then the original competition winner would be allowed—indeed expected—to carry out this extra work.

Stripped of its official phraseology, this meant that the Public Works Ministry had, in fact, already decided on a *permanent* narrowing of the entrances to the lagoon, with, *perhaps*, the addition at a later date of a mobile system to close the entrances completely when needed. How it reached this decision remains a mystery, but we can speculate. The fourth sub-committee had split almost equally into two groups—one for permanent narrowing, one for a mobile system. By opting for permanent narrowing *and* (albeit later) a mobile system, the Ministry achieved that classic bureaucratic compromise, one which it believed would satisfy everyone and, more important, protect itself from the risk of censure from the government.

Reaction was immediate. The influential London publication, *Architectural Review*, which had expressed consistent concern about Venice (in May 1971 it devoted an entire issue to 'Venice: problems and possibilities') commented 'Has [the Ministry] considered what a permanent narrowing will do to the tides and their vital role of washing out the lagoon? And what about the effect of further land reclamation (which a permanent narrowing is bound to entail) on the delicate ecological balance of the lagoon . . . The international group of experts recently convened by UNESCO . . .

expressed its strong disapproval of the Italian government's apparent inability to tackle such a fundamental problem . . . While the responsible Italian authorities create more and more confusion over a matter of such prime importance, the rest of the world must wonder despairingly whether a repeat of the events of November 1966 is not the only way of galvanizing those authorities into action.'

There were other complaints about the conditions of the competition. A major one was that it was both a competition and a request for tenders. This meant that the lone engineer, architect, or designer was excluded unless he could form a consortium with a large company capable of tendering for, and, if successful, carrying out the contract. Next, the entries for the competition would be assessed by a committee nominated by the Minister for Public Works. This committee would be entitled to nominate a single winner, or itself work out a scheme based on a part of this entry, a part of that, and then suggest to each of these competitors that he join the others to share the contract. The committee would then make a recommendation to the Technical and Scientific Committee appointed to advise the Italian government on administering the Special Law on Venice and to the Senior Council of the Ministry of Public Works which would express their opinion on the entry or entries. Finally, the Public Works Ministry would announce the winner or winners.

If a competitor successfully passed all these stages he would still be faced with a whole range of restrictions: penalty clauses for late completion, the fact that he would be required to keep to fixed prices, except for inflation provisions allowed by Italian law, and that if, at a later stage, the Ministry decided to go ahead with the addition of the mobile gates, the competitor would be required to carry out this work at the price quoted in the original tender, subject again only to revision as allowed by Italian law. A respected London group of consulting engineers, who had intended to enter the competition, announced after studying the conditions: 'To win this competition would be to take a quick passage to bankruptcy. We cannot believe that the Italian government is serious.'

For Frassetto and his colleagues at the Institute, the government's decision to opt for a permanent narrowing of the lagoon's entrances was inexplicable. His own conclusions about the lagoon, reached after five years of painstaking scientific study, appeared to have been totally ignored. So, on 6 November 1975, he sat down at his desk and set out in three concisely written pages everything he saw to be scientifically wrong with the Ministry's decision. Well aware that what he was doing would hardly advance his career, he handed his 'intervention', as he calls it, to the UNESCO office in Venice and then released it publicly.

It made a damning case against the government's plans. If a system of permanently narrowing the entrances of the lagoon were to work—that is if the entrances were to be reduced sufficiently to prevent the Adriatic rushing in at flood times—then it would be necessary to fill in the 1,000 yards wide Lido entrance for all but 150 yards, and narrow the 500 yards wide Chioggia entrance to 70 yards. The narrower entrances would act like sluice gates, allowing the water to enter the lagoon only at a reduced rate, like a funnel with a narrow neck. But even the narrower entrances would not be able to keep out high tides which lasted longer than three hours, or which had peaks of more than 39 inches above average. Slowing down the rate the water entered the lagoon would not help with high tides of long duration, because the extra time would allow all the water to get in eventually. Tides higher than average would force the water through at a rate which would cancel out the fact that the entrances were narrower. So narrowing the entrances was only a partial solution which could have disastrous side effects.

The speed of the water through the narrower entrances would generate erosion of the sea-bed and unpredictable vortexes which could be a danger to ships passing through the lagoon. The smaller amount of seawater entering at each tide cycle would reduce the flushing action, particularly in the corners of the lagoon, such as the area between Porto Marghera and Venice.

There would be a reduction in the tide range in the northern part of the lagoon, with serious consequences, such as a lowering of the salt content of the water if the fresh water flow from the Sile river branch stream was allowed to predominate. Not only could this have unfortunate results on the ecology of the area, but it could also provide an excellent breeding ground for mosquitoes, opening up the astonishing possibility of a return of malaria, eradicated from Venice in the last century. The reduction of the volume of water over the whole lagoon which would follow the permanent narrowing of the entrances could also increase the local formation of fog—through evaporation from the shallowest areas, and from the humid *bareni*—with obvious consequences for air, sea and lagoon traffic.

Yet, as Frassetto and his Institute proved to their own satisfaction, all these problems could be avoided by using a mobile closure system, limiting the permanent narrowing of the entrances to only the few metres necessary to provide the foundations for manoeuvreable gates. Using their mathematical model and their historical data, Frassetto and his team concluded that there would be times when closing only some of the gates to narrow the entrances would be sufficient to avert flooding, and many fewer times when total closure would be necessary. They calculated that the entrances would need to be only partially closed 15 to 30 times a year, for a total time of between 100 to 400 hours: total closure they believed would only happen up to 5 times a year, for a total time of up to 30 hours. This period of total closure represents less than one per cent of the period ships would actually want to use the entrances.

Gates would provide a practical method of preventing flooding, and would not affect other aspects of the lagoon. They would neither worsen the present pollution nor change the lagoon's environmental characteristics. In short, Frassetto repeated what the Institute's five years of research had shown —that the case in favour of mobile gates and against a permanent narrowing of the lagoon entrances was an overwhelming one. But if the Italian government noticed Frassetto's views, then it was not impressed by them. His report was met with an enigmatic silence.

By 1975 Frassetto had become an embarrassment to the Italian government. He was promoted, out of the way, and a new director was appointed to head the Institute in Venice. Frassetto is a loyal and patriotic Italian, so when he spoke to us about his term of office he tended to emphasize the positive aspects of what he had achieved.

We now understand the forces at work in Venice and we know how to act to save it for ten, twenty-five or fifty years. We can't pretend, however, that the solutions we offer are final; every generation will have to do its bit. But we have to begin now, because if we don't then there is no doubt that the next generation will be too late. I left the Institute because I felt that the time had come for science to hand over our first efforts to the technical people. Then they can get on with saving Venice for the next ten to fifty years while science moves to the long term investigation needed to save it for the next thousand years.

In seeking the information he needed to give Venice a six-hour flood warning, Frassetto found that Venice triggered other studies of worldwide climatological and oceanographical problems. So from applied research in Venice, he moved to fundamental research, and began to work on marine environment for the CNR, and, on a wider scale, to contribute to GARP (Global Atmospheric Research Programme), an international investigation into the world's climate and its causes.

But his concern for Venice was too deep for him to be able to quit completely, or to disguise his bitterness.

You cannot write off six years just like that. I will always be at the service of reasonable and honest people and I intend to continue to make my contribution to try to save Venice. I refuse to be eliminated because I do not belong to a political current. I belong to a scientific current, and I cannot be conditioned into silence or into allowing scientific truth to be manipulated for political ends.

Why had the scientific knowledge of how to save Venice failed to become a political reality?

There is an illness in government today, and Italy has it worse than most. When a politician takes power then he must also take responsibility. The pleasures of power are among the rewards for taking that responsibility. But in Italy the people who take power decline responsibility. This happens at all levels of government. So for these people there is only one reaction when they are faced with the responsibility of making a decision. They avoid it. They either criticize the proposal so as to justify doing nothing, or if pushed for an answer they say no, because it involves less immediate risk not to do something than to go ahead and do it.

But there are some things that require doing straight away. Agreed, there is a risk in doing them. Every action has a risk. You can reduce this risk, by taking proper advice, but in the end you have to take a decision and pay for it if it is wrong or get the glory for it if it is right. In Italy it is hard to find anyone in government who thinks this way. It is hard to find anyone who has the power to say yes and the courage to do so. No decision can be taken without criticism, lengthy discussions, and the intervention of a great mass of ignorant people. You can't even confine the discussion to prepared people. Must equal weight be given to ignorance as to the judgement and scientific skill acquired by a lifetime of preparation?

Politicians are often afraid of scientific truths. They are so locked into their own immediate interests they cannot see beyond today. They have no time to look to the future. They have no time for scientific advice about the future. They delude themselves that by repairing past damage they are saving Venice, when they need to act now to save Venice for tomorrow. But they are afraid to act for fear of the unknown. They say 'If we do this, what will happen in the long term?' There is only one certainty about the long term—if they continue to do nothing, Venice will die.

Postscript

By the mid 1970s Venice was only one example among many of the inability of Italian administration to cope with the nation's problems, but it was the most spectacular. The Venetians themselves had begun to show impatience in 1975, when the Christian Democratic vote fell by just enough to make possible a coalition government between the Socialists and the Communists—the city's first left-wing government since 1947.

But the local politicians could do nothing fundamental without the help of Rome. And in Rome virtually nothing was done. The malaise which led the lire to plunge in value in the spring of 1976, and which had made possible the huge bribes to politicians by aircraft and oil companies, not to mention the CIA, had thoroughly infected the business of saving Venice too. Anyway, inflation had made a mockery of the huge sums the Italian Parliament had voted three years earlier. Politically, Venice had become an embarrassment. As Peter Nichols, who is the Rome correspondent of *The Times* of London, writes, 'A straightforward Italian politician asked straightforwardly yes or no would agree that probably the best thing that could happen to Venice would be that it would sink, and the sooner the better.'

This certainly seemed to be the attitude in Rome. In fact

one of the last acts of the Christian Democratic Government before it finally fell in May 1976, was to hustle through Parliament a law cancelling all the anti-pollution regulations—including those imposed on the Porto Marghera and Mestre industrialists by the Special Law to Save Venice. A new set of regulations were announced but the industrialists were given until 1985 to comply with them. As well, all court actions pending against them for breaches of the anti-pollution laws they had already committed were ordered to be dropped.

Rome's attitude, so typically expressed in this action, made the great debate about the role of the Italian Communist Party in the nation's government seem irrelevant to Venice. It would take a miracle, not Marxism, to save the city. Only one question remained unanswered: how long would it take to die?

Of course, Venice could go with a bang, as it almost did in 1966. In the decade after that disaster only one fundamental change had been made; next time the city would be warned. But a warning would not be enough to save it if the climatic conditions combined to produce a third wave of high tide. Venice is too vulnerable to withstand that.

We think it more likely that it will die less dramatically: not with a bang but a whimper. And anyone finding this forecast far-fetched can quickly learn to suspend their disbelief by taking one of the big ferries from the Riva degli Schiavoni—or the motor launch which leaves Harry's Bar every day at noon—and going to the lagoon island, Torcello, beyond Murano and Burano.

Torcello was the first island of the lagoon to be inhabited because it was the most convenient to flee to from the barbarian Huns. By the tenth century the inhabitants had adjusted to a lagoon life which was not to change for centuries: they were fishermen and traders, whose livelihood and security both depended on the water. They were adventurous too, and pushed East to find new markets for their trade. The cathedral at Torcello with its melancholy Virgin is one of the first great examples of Byzantine art in western Europe.

The rise and fall of Torcello inspired James Morris to some of the most evocative prose in his book on Venice.

The city flourished and grew for some centuries, and by the 1500s is said to have had 20,000 inhabitants, a score of splendid churches, paved streets and many bridges . . . The two pious merchants who stole the body of St Mark from the Egyptians were both citizens of Torcello. Torcello had her own gateway to the sea, through Cavallino, and was a flourishing mart and shipping centre in her own right . . . In the twelfth century one commentator wrote respectfully of the '*Magnum Emporium Torcellanorum*'.

She then entered a disastrous decline. Her canals were clogged up with silt from the rivers, not yet diverted from the lagoon, and her people were decimated by malaria and pestilent fevers. Her trade was killed at last by the rising energy of the Rialto islands, better placed in the centre of the lagoon, near the mouth of the Brenta. Torcello fell into lethargy and despondence. Her most vigorous citizens moved to Venice, her merchant houses folded and were forgotten. Presently the island was so deserted and disused that Venetian builders, when they were short of materials, used to come to Torcello and load the remains of palaces into their barges, scrabbling among the ruins for the right size of staircase or a suitably sculptured cornice. Through the centuries poor Torcello rotted, crumbling and sub-siding and declining into marshland again. When Napoleon overthrew the Republic, she proclaimed herself, in a moment of frantic virility, an autonomous State; but by the middle of the nineteenth century a visit to Torcello was, for every romantic visitor, a positive ecstasy of melancholia.

Now Torcello and the lagoon around it has become some-thing else; a case history of how impermanent a city in the lagoon can be. Not far from Torcello the islands of Constan-ziaca and Ammiana have not even survived above the water. Constanziaca disappeared at the end of the seventeenth century with all its monasteries and churches and is remem-bered only as a small outcrop in the lagoon, on which the bones of dead Venetians, for whom there was no longer any room in the cemetery of San Michele, were dumped.

Torcello did not physically disappear. It declined because another lagoon island was made secure from the barbarians and took its place as the centre of industry, commerce and social life. For over a thousand years after the centre of gravity in the lagoon shifted from Torcello to the Riva Alto (or high, right bank of the Grand Canal, which became known as the Rialto) it remained there. Only in the past twenty-five years has that centre of gravity begun to move again.

It is moving with remarkable speed to Mestre and Porto Marghera, and this is what will lead inexorably to the death of Venice. The money and the political will to reverse the trend are simply not there. We believe that the process will be so rapid that our children will be the last to see Venice as we know it. Already the city abounds with clues about the way it will go, and it is easy to create a scenario for the last days of Venice.

It begins with housing, when the local council becomes impatient at the delays and restrictions on development, and builds instead in the new suburbs of Mestre, where most Venetians have close relations or old neighbours. As the population of Mestre grows and the historic centre's declines, the municipal services become concentrated on the mainland. More public departments and private industries move their headquarters from the city, following the lead of the Venetian Chamber of Commerce, which shifted its offices to Mestre in 1975. The quality of Venice's services, like postal deliveries and rubbish collection, deteriorates. There is no further need for deep canals, which are allowed to silt up, just as they did in Torcello. Although gondolas might have a shallow enough draught to get by, there are no Venetians to repair or row them (already these occupations do not provide a proper living). Finally, those ordinary Venetians who had chosen to stay in the city conclude that since they have to make the journey to Mestre so often, to fill in forms or get medical treatment, or to see their children's teachers, they might as well move there themselves.

The poor working class areas of Canareggio behind the station and Castello around the derelict Arsenale are the first to crumble away; old streets are closed because of falling masonry; the houses and *palazzi* are boarded up, and rot away. The remaining rich Venetians concentrate in smaller areas of the city. As the population falls, congregations become too small and more churches are closed: St Mark's and the Frari are among the few to stay open. San Giovanni e Paolo closes soon after the hospital next door is moved to the mainland. Even the interior of the opera house, La

Fenice, is dismantled and reconstructed in the shell of a cinema in Mestre.

Each summer the tourists flood back in, like an *acqua alta* in November, and for a few months the shutters are opened, and life is breathed into the historic centre again. But not for long, because luxury hotels like the Danieli begin to find the cost of opening for just a few months prohibitive, with wages high and strikes even more common: losses in Venice eat into the profits their new branches are making in Mestre. The Gritti, of course, had begun to close for the winter in 1973.

The tourists tend to stay in new hotels in Mestre; they cross the causeway each morning and tramp around echoing streets, eating their sandwich lunches, hoping that enough of the old buildings remain open to give them some shade from the sun, and complaining about the gaps in the Grand Canal, where whole *palazzi* have been removed, like pulled teeth, and rebuilt in the public gardens in Bochum, at Disneyland in Florida, in Fukuoka, or overlooking Sydney Harbour.

As the sun sets it is time to go back for an evening meal in Mestre, or Venezia Nuova as it is known, to distinguish it from Venezia Vecchia, or the tourist island of old Venice. After dinner visitors are able to go to the mainland branch of Florian's, a perfect reproduction of the original, and plan the next day's round of the new museums which house the nucleus of the great collection of paintings from the Ducal Palace and the Accademia—removed to keep them safe from the growing damp and humidity. And there they might overhear an old man describe what Venezia Vecchia was like to those who had come too late to see for themselves.

Index

Index

Index

Cicogna, Countess Anna Maria, 98, 103
Clarke, Sir Ashley, 88, 99, 108; San Nicolo restoration, 131–6, 138; stone restoration, paper on, 154; & Tintoretto paintings, 111; VAT issue, 101–2
Colombo, Emilio, 61
Comitato Italiano per Venezia, 130
Comitato per il Centro Storico Ebraico di Venezia, 129
Commission to Safeguard Venice, 53–4, 95, 104
Commoner, Barry, 134
Communist Party, 75–7, 87–8, 177
Consorzio di Credito per le Opere Publiche (Crediop), 59–70
Constanziaca island: submerged, 180
Conti, Corrado, 67–8
Corriere della Sera, 50, 105
Cortese, Marino, 99–100
Customs House, 128, 129

Dandolo, Doge Enrico, 12
Danieli hotel, 121, 181
Dorigo, Vladimiro, 91–2
Ducal Palace, 73–4, 182; flood, 25, 26; Porta della Carta, 112, 114; Tintoretto paintings, anti-Collegio, 111, 114

Eurodollar market loans, 59, 62, 68

Fenice, La, 105, 181–2
Ferrante, Ferrucio, 79
Financial Times, 60, 68
floods and flooding, 30, 34, 40–1, 46, 158; control & warnings, 163, 174, 175; forecast model, 161; 1966 flood, 25–7; government action, 30–1, 50, 94; recovery, apparent speed of, 28; *see also* lagoon, Special Laws, UNESCO
Florence: flood damage, 26–8, 140
Florian's café, 28, 182
Forte di Sant'Andrea, 109–10, 113
Fortuny de Madrazo, Mariano, 22
Frassetto, Roberto, 156–62; 'mobile closure system', 163–5, 167–8,

172–4; on illness in government, 175–6
French Committee, 128–9

Gazzettino, 83, 105
German National Commission, 128
Gibson, Bethune, 150
Giudecca canal area, 45, 82, 84, 87
Global Atmosphere Research Programme (GARP), 175
gondola industry, 76, 105, 159, 181
Gozzi, Carlo, 73
Grand Canal, 17, 18, 73, 76, 85, 87, 108, 130, 137, 151, 180, 182
Gray, Col. James A., 70, 118–24
Guardian, 62–4
Guggenheim, Peggy, 87

Hale, John, 109–10, 113
Hempel, Kenneth, 112, 114, 155; stone cleaning, 149–51; stone preservation, 151–2; stone restoration diagnosis, 140–9, 154
Herwarth, Hans von, 98, 128
Hitchins, Graham, 135–6
housing, 16–17, 20, 47, 58, 80, 84–6, 131, 181; 'parking houses', 85; redevelopment plans, 82, 84, 89

Ilva steel works, 38
indirizzi development plan (1975), 51, 54–8, 97
industrial zones, 1st & 2nd, 29–30, 32, 36–40, 44, 52; third, 38, 55–8, 97; *see also* Porto Marghera
Institute for the Study of the Dynamics of Grand Masses (1969), 156–61, 174; lagoon closure competition, 163ff.
International Centre for Conservation and Restoration, Rome, 146
International Consultative Committee to Save Venice, 56, 95–8, 154; meeting (1974), 98–103
International Fund for Monuments (IFM): Venice Committee projects, 118–21, 124; Venice office, 121, 124; *see also* pigeons
Italia Nostra (1959), 130

186

Index

Saint Erasmo island, 26, 38
St Mark's Cathedral, 11, 12, 19, 127; fabric decay, 21–2, 112–13; flood, 25; Gothic arch, 112; Zen chapel, 22
St Mark's Square, 12, 129; flood, 25, 26, 28; Loggetta, 107, 112; subsidence, 43; waterfront collision risk, 45
Saloni warehouse, Zattere, 104
Salva, Paolo Rosa, 46
San Giorgio Maggiore island, 98, 102
San Gregorio laboratory, 111
sanitation and sewage, 34, 51, 52, 163, 170, 173
Sarti, Adolfo, 56, 98, 100
SAVA aluminium plant, 38
Save Venice Inc., 31, 114–18
Save Venice laws; see Special Laws
Save Venice voluntary groups, 53, 64, 84–5, 94, 107ff.; fund raising & VAT, 31, 70, 101–2; national groups: American, 31, 114–24; British, 31, 83, 88, 107–14, 133–139; French, 128; German, 125, 128; Italian, 129–30; others, 129
Scaglione, Dominic, 65
Scano, Luigi, 58
Scarpa, Father (San Nicolo church), 132, 137–8, 139
Scarpi, Father (Santa Teresa church), 23
Schola Canton, 121; Grande Tedesca, 125–8; Italiana, 129
'scirocco' wind, 25, 160
Scuola dei Carmini, 121
    di San Giovanni Evangelista, 120, 124
    di San Marco, 20
    di San Rocco, 119, 124
    Grande della Misericordia, 19
sea defence system, walls and dykes, 26, 28, 30, 109; creation of, 34–5; government inertia, 35–6; government spending on, 50; indirizzi plans for, 57; 1907 Act, 35; 'zone of respect', 36
Shylock (Merchant of Venice), 13, 124–5

Social Democrat Party, 46, 75, 77–8
Socialist Party, 75–8, 88, 177
Societa Dante Alighieri, 129
Special Laws: (1937–56), 50, 66; (1966), 31, 50; (1973), 50–5, 58, 72, 96, 104; Grand Committee & lagoon closure, 167–8, 171; loan contract (1971), 31, 61, 63; Crediop Eurodollar loan (1973), 59–71, 80, 97, 100; Technical & Scientific Committee, 54, 171
statues and monuments, 19, 20, 22, 43, 95, 96, 107, 112, 128, 136–7, 139, 140–1; cleaning techniques, 149–50, 152
Stochetti, General, 58
stone preservation: cleaning techniques, 149–53; conservation methods, 151–2; decay analysis, 140–9, 154–5; manpower career problems, 152–5
subsidence, 158, 163; core drilling, 161–2; 'fixed heads', 42–5
sulphur dioxide pollution; see under pollution
Sunday Times, 82–3, 84

Teotoca Madonna mosaic, Torcello, 113
The Times, 37, 64, 66, 71–2, 177
Thorneycroft, Lady, 112
Tides Forecast Office, 161
Tiepolo: Scalzi ceiling, 18
Tintoretto, 13; Ducal Palace paintings, 111; Scuola di San Rocco paintings, 119
Tomellieri, Angelo, 95, 99
Torcello island, 11, 178–9; cathedral mosaics, 113
Torraca, Giorgio, 146, 147, 155
tourist trade, 12–14, 47, 90, 91, 182
town planning controversy, 78–92, 104; Communist involvement, 87; zonal divisions, 82, 84, 86, 90, 97
trained craftsmen, shortage of, 105–106, 152–5
Trattoria al Giardinetto, 20

UNESCO, 156–7; flood damage,